Practical guide to

BONSAI
STYLES

of the world

Practical guide to
BONSAI
STYLES
of the world

Charles S. Ceronio

BRIZA

Published by
BRIZA PUBLICATIONS
CK 1990/011690/23

BRIZA
www.briza.co.za

PO Box 11050
Queenswood 0121
Pretoria
South Africa

First edition, first impression 2015

ISBN 978-1-920217-49-5

Project manager: Reneé Ferreira
Cover design: Ronelle Oosthuizen
Inside design and typesetting: Ronelle Oosthuizen
Reproduction: Resolution Colour, Cape Town
Printed and bound by Tien Wah Press (Pte.) Ltd, Malaysia

This publication is dedicated to the three women in my life –

To my beloved wife Elsie, whose support, understanding, friendship, devotion and love over many bonsai-related years, is deeply appreciated. Thank you also for all the hours you spent, sometimes until late at night, entering, re-entering and refining the written data for the first edition.
A bouquet of sunflowers to you 'Mams'.

To my daughter Elvira for your 'critical eye' and appreciated suggestions – I do love you.

To my late mother from whom I inherited my love for flora in particular, and nature in general – I honour you in beloved memory.

Contents

PART 1
The art of bonsai

PART 2
Bonsai styles

Preface

Bonsai is a living tree, or a group of trees, which is grown in a suitable container on a miniature scale. It possesses the natural beauty of a fully grown tree, but is artistically created to achieve a total aesthetic impact.

Over the last few decades, the worldwide popularity of bonsai increased rapidly, possibly due to the technical advancement in global communications and transport. The art of bonsai as established in Japan is also found in Europe, the United States, Canada, South America, Australia, the Middle East and on the continent of Africa. Thousands of bonsai enthusiasts travel regularly to Japan to witness the art of bonsai cultivated the Japanese way.

Numerous books and visual aids are available, not just in Japanese and English, but also in other languages. These days it is not unusual for a bonsai instructor to travel to other countries to guide, teach, and exchange bonsai expertise with host bonsai organisations.

The majority of the bonsai books in circulation generally cover matters such as history, cultivating techniques, designing and training principles, general care and maintenance and propagation techniques. In other words, these books teach the reader the basic techniques of bonsai art. Designing and styling, on the other hand, are challenging techniques; perhaps somewhat difficult to master. However, it is essential that the reader should master these techniques in order to train plant material into quality bonsai.

The natural tree, which bonsai emulates, grows into various characteristic forms. Factors such as variation in plant species or geological, climatic and regional variations, all have an influence on the shape of a tree. By studying the various tree forms, the bonsai artist is able to take an untrained plant and copy one of nature's forms: this process is called styling.

There is a great need for a book – or perhaps books – that specifically places the emphasis on bonsai styles. Such a book could serve everyone who is interested in cultivating bonsai, as a guide to styling trees and to classifying the various bonsai styles.

Charles Ceronio, who has since 1968 experience in growing bonsai, is well aware of this need. Furthermore, he is not only an accomplished bonsai artist, but also an outstanding illustrator. For instance, he has expertly and in detail sketched numerous tree styles to supplement the practical information contained in this book. It is quite amazing how a small change in the curvature of a trunk line, or a branch line, transforms a tree into an entirely new style.

I have met Charles on several bonsai-related occasions. While on a visit to South Africa in 1991, he and his wife, Elsie, and their daughter, Elvira, received me hospitably in their home. On that occasion I established a wonderful friendship with them.

Without hesitation, I accepted a request by Charles to write a preface to this book. I am honoured to be associated with his writing of this book, and hereby extend my congratulations and best wishes to Charles and his family on the accomplishment of this new venture.

Roy K. Nagatoshi

Acknowledgements

To all the great masters who have crossed my path on my journey through life and from whom I have had the privilege to learn more about the art of bonsai, I humbly bow to your much appreciated superior knowledge.

Thank you, my old friends John and Alice Naka for your tuition, influence and inspiration since our first meeting in 1980 and on the follow-up visits you made to South Africa. Thank you also for the warm reception at your home in Los Angeles during the 25th anniversary of the Californian Bonsai Society in 1982. You contributed in opening the art of bonsai to many of us Westerners and we salute you for your mastership.

To the great masters, thank your for what I personally could learn from you: Ben Oki, Melba Tucker, Vaughn Banting, Roy Nagatoshi, Shigeo Kato, Deborah Korreshoff and others. Please forgive me if I erroneously omitted someone from this esteemed list.

Thank you, Bill Valavanis for being an exceptionally gifted tutor, among others through your fine articles in *International Bonsai*. It was as a result of these articles that I was inspired to write this book.

To my co-tutor and friend, Roy Nagatoshi, for your kind and inspiring preface and for all the knowledge and useful hints we as South Africans could gain from your lectures and demonstrations during your visits to our country.

I also wish to express my sincere thanks and appreciation to the following people who in some way or another helped to make this publication possible:

- Dr Koos le Roux for his enthusiasm and drive during the initial phase of the project as well as for his assistance with the chapter on the artistic aspects of bonsai.
- My sincere thanks and appreciation to my dear friend and patron of the World bonsai Friendship Association, the late Mr Diazo Iwasaki, for allowing me to use some of the photographs of his world-class bonsai collection.
- To Mr Fusazo Takeyama for the use of the photographs of his *Zelkova serrata*.
- To Robert Steven for the use of some of his photographs and sketches (especially on the windswept style).
- To Mr Luu Truongson for permission to use his inspiring photographs of the various Chinese styles.
- Thank you also to Erik Wigert of Wigert's Bonsai in Florida and to Mr Thanun Thanun for the use of their photographs.
- To my friends, Leong Kwang, Chase Rosade and Aslam Sulaiman for allowing me to use their photographs.
- To all the local bonsai friends for granting permission to use photographs of their prizewinning trees.
- Dot Thompson for her valuable contribution in editing and refining of the first edition of the book and to Reneé Ferreira in editing and refining this third edition of the book.

Lastly, and most importantly, I am grateful to my Creator for opening my eyes to the beauty of His creation and for instilling in me the desire to share this love with my fellow humans.

Introduction

Japanese philosophy states:

*Respect all the rules under the sun,
but use all the freedom under the rules.*

With the above philosophy in mind, I have written this book on bonsai styles: firstly, to arouse the interest of bonsai enthusiasts in creating their own masterpieces; secondly, to make bonsai enthusiasts aware of the numerous tree forms that are found in various parts of the world; and thirdly, to introduce my series of African bonsai styles, which I was inspired to develop when I became aware of the importance of style.

It is my wish that this book will not only serve as a practical guide to styling, but also as a source of reference on the bonsai styles that are found worldwide, for which a great need exists at most bonsai clubs.

Having said that, the reader should not adhere rigidly to the do's and don'ts of styling, but should rather draw inspiration from local trees and shrubs, as a more natural approach is beginning to take root.

I hope that this book will inspire and stimulate the mind of the reader, and that it will contribute towards the enjoyment of bonsai by enthusiasts all over the world.

Charles Ceronio

Pretoria
South Africa

PART 1
The art

of bonsai

Webster's Dictionary defines art as –

'the power of performing certain actions, especially as acquired by experience, study, or observation', or

'the conscious use of skill, taste and creative imagination in the practical definition or production of beauty', or

'the product of skill and taste according to aesthetic principles.'

According to these definitions, bonsai may be regarded as a skilful and creative art form. Therefore, a true masterpiece should reflect grace, character, dignity, movement or whatever element the artist wishes to express in his creation.

Bonsai and the floral art of ikebana are Japan's foremost cultural and horticultural art forms. Although it is not regarded as one of the fine arts, bonsai is certainly an art form – one that involves living material, which is unique in the world of art.

The creation of a bonsai masterpiece may be compared with creating a sculpture, but sculpturing with living plant material. It is therefore a dynamic, ongoing process and never a completed work of art.

Similar to other art forms, imagination and creative skill are required for the production of a bonsai masterpiece.

A true 'bonsai master' possesses the same artistic talents and skills as a Michelangelo, Rembrandt, Eduardo Villa, Bach, Beethoven or any other great master. These artists distinguished themselves from the ordinary pavement artists by creating timeless works of art.

An artist's imagination, sense of reality, emotions and passion to express beauty and display craftsmanship all have an influence on his creations. In addition, the creative process requires that the artist uses his sensory perception of texture, rhythm, line movement, and so forth. Only a true bonsai artist can create a masterpiece that evokes a definite mood or an atmosphere that tells a story.

Bonsai composition and design

Composition can be defined as the arrangement of artistic elements into a satisfactory visual unit.

In our context, composition and design can be described as the difference between a bonsai tree and a potted plant. When composition and design are translated into bonsai styles, natural chaos is transformed into visual order.

Design is, of course, an extremely personal matter that involves the artist's own creative experience, opinion and taste. No definite rules apply – there are no do's and don'ts. The natural born artist intuitively does the right thing, giving heed to the advice of no one. The true artist is capable of expressing emotion, harmony, balance, rhythm and other elements of composition and design.

However, all bonsai growers strive for originality. Originality in this instance may be defined as giving expression to one's own impression of nature by way of a scaled-down bonsai tree. One must therefore study and observe tree forms in their natural habitat before one can 'design' a tree.

The creative ability of a bonsai grower will be influenced by many factors:

- examples set by nature, the use of common sense, and the application of basic horticultural principles;
- exposure to beginner classes, demonstrations, symposia, conventions, role model bonsai artists, and so forth;
- knowledge of Eastern philosophy and art (which could assist the bonsai grower in the expression of simplicity and austere sublimity);
- endowment with natural artistic ability; and
- matured bonsai taste.

Schematically, this creative process can be illustrated as follows:

Trees in nature

Artist's impression of nature *plus* other influences such as culture, society and religion

Individual's impression of nature (personal elements added)

15

Basic art concepts applicable to bonsai

Basic art principles, such as line movement, form and shape are used in creating a bonsai. Line movement can consist of various lines and curves. Normally two-dimensional lines are used for creating forms on a flat surface. A flat surface can be converted three-dimensionally to create depth of field.

At this stage colour and texture are introduced into the created space, but the result of the action does not necessarily produce a work of art – the above principles should be rearranged to form an aesthetically pleasing integration of artistic elements.

The ten principles for creating a work of art are: impact, focal point, proportion, depth of field, harmony, line movement, rhythm, balance, silhouette and contrast. We will now look at each of these elements in more detail.

The ten principles for creating a work of art are:

- impact
- focal point
- proportion
- depth of field
- harmony
- line movement
- rhythm
- balance
- silhouette and
- contrast.

This super masterpiece, called 'Buryu' or Dancing Dragon, was refined by the famous Masahiko Kimura. It is a Shimpaku juniper in the driftwood style that belonged to the late Mr Iwasaki.

Impact

Impact is the split second realisation that the tree in view is either a masterpiece or just another tree in a pot. This first impression is due to the culmination of positive factors in the creative process. At this stage the tree is evaluated in totality.

One's first impression of masterpiece bonsai is one of strength and beauty, because aspects of movement, balance, depth, rhythm and beauty are present.

Focal point

A good design has a strong focal point towards which the eye is drawn automatically. A tree without a strong focal point is without character and just another tree. Too many focal points, on the other hand would distract from the beauty and impact of the tree.

Let us look at some examples of strong focal points:

- Roots
- Trunk and tree shape
- Special trunk effects
- Unusual branch formations
- Seasonal changes, colour, fruit and flowers

Roots

Strong and powerful anchoring surface roots which fuse with the trunk can be an interesting focal point.

Exposed roots: on a dramatic exposed-root style, the strange twisted exposed roots are without doubt a strong focal point.

Root-over-rock style: the roots crawling over and fusing with the rock undoubtedly form a focal point of this fascinating style.

Trunk and tree shape

The focal point of this baobab tree is its overpowering thick trunk.

The delicate trunk of the literati style and the smooth trunk of the broom style form their unique focal points.

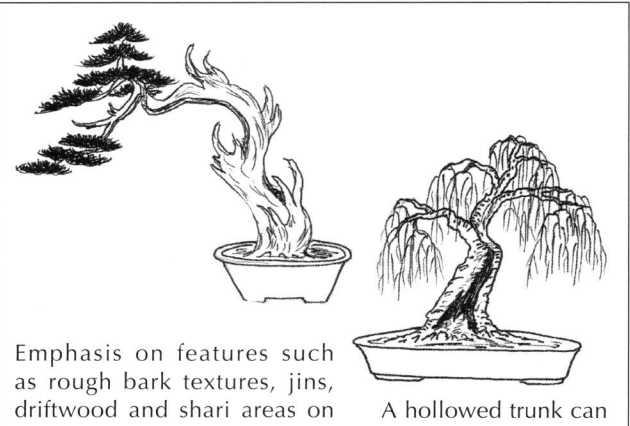

The unusual and sometimes twisted trunk of the Horai styled tree forms its focal point.

Special trunk effects

Emphasis on features such as rough bark textures, jins, driftwood and shari areas on the lower part of the trunk contributes not only towards the aesthetic beauty but also creates a dramatic focal point.

A hollowed trunk can be a very interesting focal point.

Unusual branch formations

The zigzag branch pattern of the Pierneef styled tree forms the focal point of this composition.

Seasonal changes, colour, fruit and flowers

The effect of seasonal changes in delicate deciduous trees, colourful berries, fruit or flowers form an interesting focal point.

In this tree the interesting trunk forms the focal point. The tree is from the collection of the late Mr Iwasaki.

Proportion

Proportion is the ratio to which the trunk, main branches, secondary and tertiary branches are related to form a harmonious unit. It is important to study tree forms in nature in order to understand the relationship between a tree's height, the trunk's width, the branch formations, etc.

Trunk size

The ideal proportion between the trunk's width and the height of the tree is a ratio of 1:6. For example, if the trunk's diameter, in the case of a formal upright tree, is 8 cm, the trunk's length would be approximately 48 cm. The trunk should also taper towards the apex.

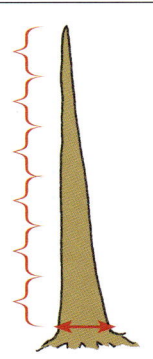

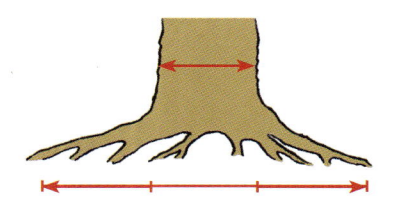

The root base should normally be twice or three times the size of the trunk. These dimensions are applicable to almost all the styles except to the baobab, which normally does not have a wide root spread.

In the case of the baobab style where the trunk's width is the focal point, the ratio between the trunk's diameter towards the height of the tree can vary from 1:2 to 1:3.

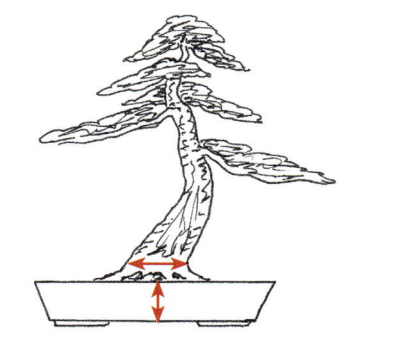

The trunk's diameter usually equals the container's depth. The thicker the trunk, the deeper the pot and vice versa.

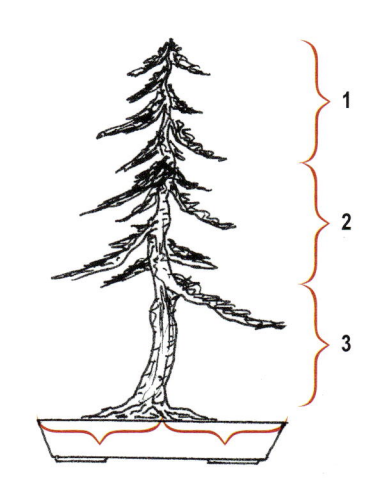

The length of the pot is normally one-third shorter than that of the trunk or in the ratio of 2:3.

Branch proportion

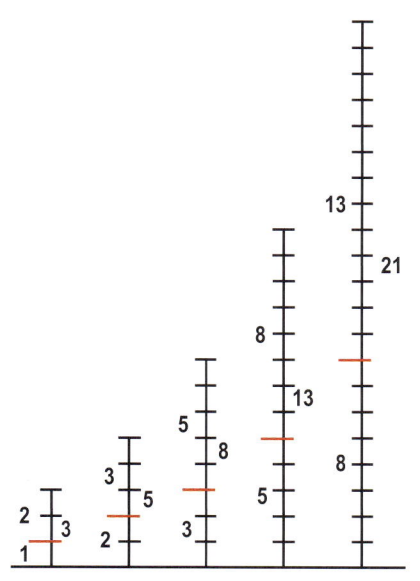

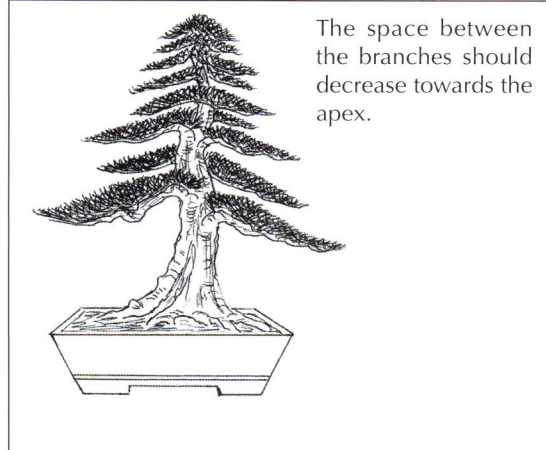

The length of a container for a short tree with wide branches can therefore be in the ratio of 2:3.

The placement of the first branch can be done according to the Fibonacci sequence. The ratios are: 1:2, 2:3, 3:5, 5:8, 8:13, etc. If, for example, the trunk is 8 cm tall, the first branch, according to the ratio of 3:5, is placed at the height of 30 cm. The balance of 50 cm is left for the rest of the branch structure.

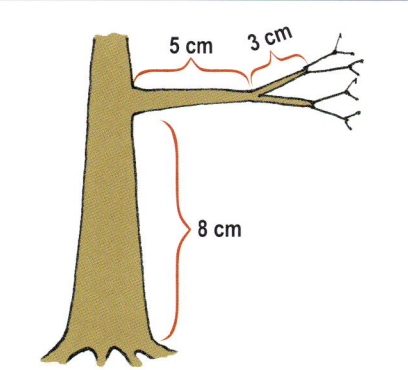

The space between the branches should decrease towards the apex.

The construction of a tree

A tree can also be constructed according to the ratio of 1:2, 2:3, 3:5, etc. If, for example, the trunk is 8 cm long, the major branches should be 5 cm with the secondary branches reduced to 3 cm, etc.

Fruit, berries and flowers

When selecting bonsai material, it is necessary to select plants with small-sized fruit, berries and flowers, as these do not reduce in size, i.e. persimmon or orange look out of proportion on a small tree.

Depth of field

Bonsai is a living art form and should therefore always be created three dimensionally. A bonsai can be compared with a cube, which has six planes:

- back and front (D and B);
- left and right (C and E); and
- top and a bottom (F and A).

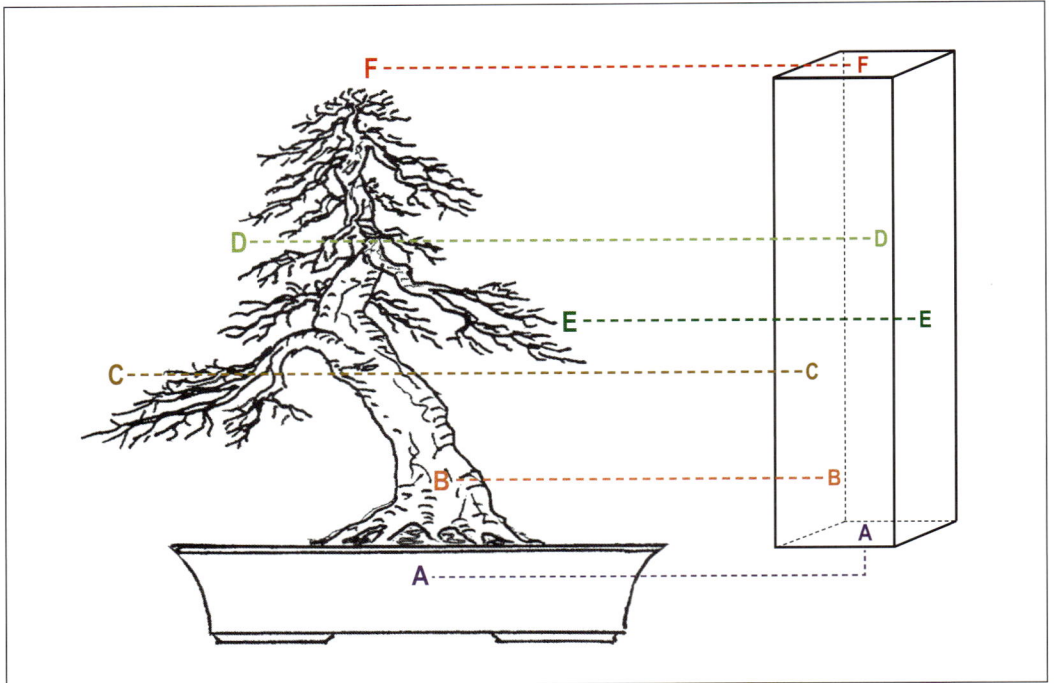

In the case of a bonsai, the side branches should be longer than the back and front branches, and the front branches should be the shortest.

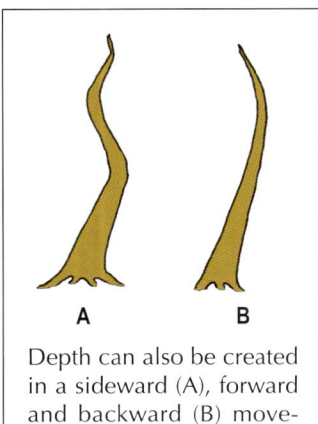

A   **B**

Depth can also be created in a sideward (A), forward and backward (B) movement of the trunk.

In the twin and double, as well as the triple and five-trunk styles, the trees should not be placed directly alongside each other but rather towards the front and the back to create depth.

Harmony

Harmony is considered to be the most important element of a creation of art. It embodies all the basic art principles and when one element is out of place the general effect will not be aesthetically pleasing, but will be found lacking in harmony.

Harmony between roots and trunk

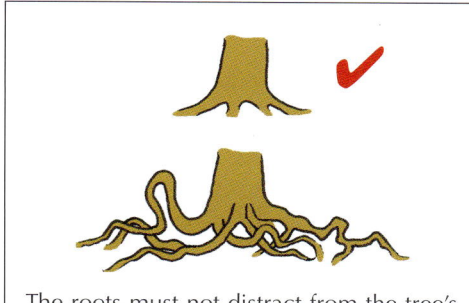

The roots must not distract from the tree's beauty, but should rather spread evenly around the trunk. Octopus-formed roots, roots crossing each other, and so on, must be avoided.

The display of roots must harmonise with the style of the tree. For instance, when a formal tree has an informal base, the two concepts are in conflict with one another, resulting in disharmony.

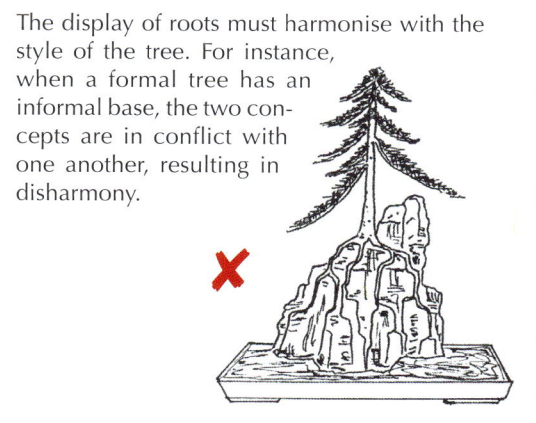

Harmony between different elements

The trunk, the branch formation and the style of the tree should be in total harmony with each other.

The style and the mood the tree is radiating should harmonise. For instance, jins would distract from the elegance of a delicate broom style and an effect of disharmony would be experienced.

Harmony between tree and container

The container must complement the tree and should not be too elaborate or overpowering. A delicate 'broom', for instance cannot be placed in a deep rectangular pot. To emphasise its smooth trunk, a shallow, light-coloured oval container should be used because it harmonises best with the slender lines of the tree.

Line movement

Line movement is very important because it radiates a certain amount of energy which could be used to good effect in the creation of a masterpiece to express a certain emotion.

The various line movements, together with the moods they symbolise, are:

- 🌿 a circle = unity
- 🌿 a vertical line = dignity
- 🌿 a horizontal line = tranquillity and calmness
- 🌿 a straight line = stability
- 🌿 a zigzag line = excitement
- 🌿 a curved line = graceful movement
- 🌿 Hogarth's line = femininity and vastness

The impact of the trunk line on the eye is clearly noticeable in Hogarth's line. In a good design the eye movement should not be allowed to wander, but is should be kept on the design itself.

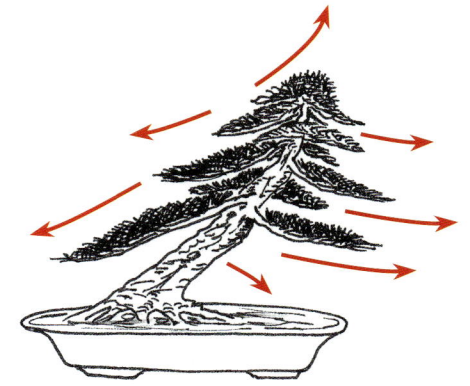

In the slanting style one can feel the tension between the opposing forces and it gives a sense of dynamism and movement to the style.

Movement can also be created by the repetitive use of motifs. Crossed lines would destroy the image of movement and should be avoided, especially in multiple trunk lines.

The trunk line clearly reflects the powerful movement that is embodied in this dramatic driftwood-style tree. The jins give further impetus to the feeling of rhythm and motion.

Rhythm

As in music, rhythm can be simulated in bonsai by using repetition of trunk and branch lines, foliage masses and negative space. It should, however, be remembered that when repetition is too regular and predictable, rhythm becomes monotonous.

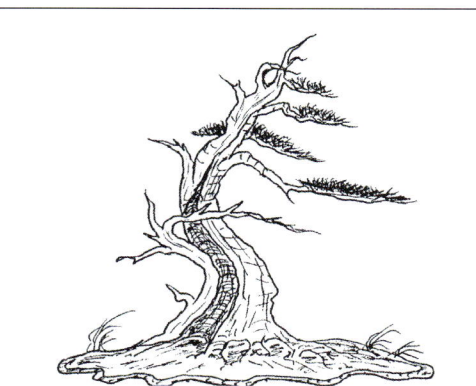

To emphasise the feeling of rhythm, all elements of a composition should lead the eye in the same direction. This aspect is clearly seen in this windswept creation. Once the basic movement in the trunk line is established, the same movement should be repeated in the branches and negative spaces. The movement is also echoed in jins and shari's.

Rhythm is created from the movement of the broad triangular foliage base to the sharp angle of the apex. The dense branch arrangement towards the apex also creates rhythm.

Line movement creates tension and energy in the design. The tree belonged to the late Mr Iwasaki.

25

Balance

Balance is one of the pillars of a successful creation of a work of art. It entails a central axis or point in the field around which the opposing forces are in equilibrium.

The following aspects play an important role in the concept of balance:

🌿 Symmetry is the simplest form of balance, but it is less exciting than asymmetrical balance, because the latter heightens the feeling of movement and rhythm.

🌿 Occult or concealed balance, on the other hand, is by far the most exiting, but it is also the most difficult to create. Although it provides greater freedom, it demands greater control and expertise. Occult balance means the control of opposing tensions through a perceived equality between the various parts in the field. These forces or tensions should be in equilibrium to create harmony and balance.

🌿 Visual weight is another important element of balance and can be described as the substance or volume of mass inside a boundary or within a silhouette line. Visual weight can either be in balance or it can dominate the one or the other side. This dominance may be used to create movement in the creation.

Symmetrical balance

The broom and formal upright styles are perfect examples of symmetrical balance. The visual weight, consisting of branches and foliage, is distributed equally to both sides of the trunk.

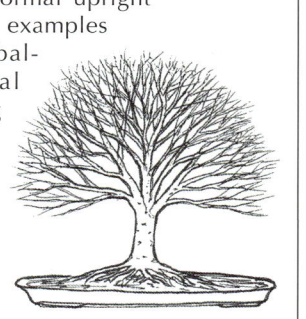

Asymmetrical balance

The tree in this sketch is a clear example of the overwhelming distribution of weight to the left-hand side. It is, however, balanced by the jinned trunks and branches on the opposite side of the centre line.

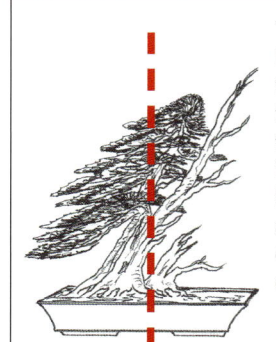

Radial balance

Radial balance is found in multiple plantings as most of the trunks sprout from the same root system. The composition is balanced by distributing the weight equally to both sides of the central line.

Negative space

Negative space on the right-hand side can also act as a balancing element in the composition. The visual weight on the left-hand side is balanced by the jinned branch on the right.

The choice of container

Containers often act as balancing and stabilising elements in the composition. The visual weight of both the cascade and literati styled trees is balanced by their containers.

Positioning

Positioning of a tree in a container can result in different tensions influencing the balance of the composition as shown in the following diagrams.

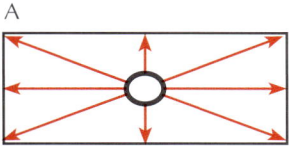

A

In diagram A the composition is too symmetrical and will be monotonous and static.

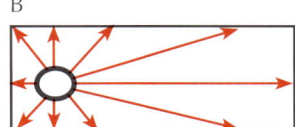

B

In diagram B the positioning of the tree is out of balance as the tension is very strongly to the right.

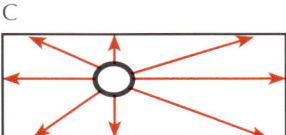

C

Diagram C is regarded the correct positioning of the tree where balance and harmony radiate in the correct positions.

Note the positioning of this baobab grown from seed by the late Theuns Roos.

27

Silhouette

A bonsai design may be appreciated for two main reasons, namely for the trunk line and the silhouette.

Most bonsai growers prefer the prominent trunk line design, although some masters grow trees, especially the pine, for their triangular silhouette only.

A densely grown Japanese black pine, with no negative spaces visible, is grown entirely for its exceptional triangular shape.

This sketch shows a slanting tree with the trunk line well visible. Negative spaces are visible between the branches as well as in the open spaces around the trunk.

Contrast

Contrast is an essential element in eliminating monotonous design and plays an important role in creating a specific mood or work of art.

Contrast can be created by using texture, colour, contour, size of flowers and berries. For example, the feathery leaves of the African thorn trees (*Senegalia* and *Vachellia* species) and *Taxodium* contrast sharply with the rough-textured bark of the trunks. The green leaves of *Olea* contrast beautifully with the greyish colour of the bark.

The orange berries of the *Pyracantha* will form an interesting contrast with a grey or blue pot. Inset: The reddish colour of the maple in autumn is in sharp contrast with the dark blue of the container.

In conclusion I would like to quote Mr Q Zhao
who is a leading bonsai grower in China:
'A bonsai is never just a natural tree reduced in size …
Shaped by human hand, bonsai is the distillation of the creator's
perception of Nature …
bonsai is the outward expression of the artist's inner life.'

There stand by Bonsai

a fragment of Nature

untroubled, serene

Loved.

Haiku
by Doug Hall

PART 2
Bonsai

styles

'And the Lord God made all kinds of trees grow out of the ground – trees that were pleasing to the eye …'

Genesis 2:9

Trees are one of God's most impressive creations, and bonsai growers throughout the world have been inspired by these masterpieces of nature to create their own bonsai masterpieces. In his book, *Bonsai Techniques I*, John Naka starts the section on different styles in bonsai by saying that '… it is fascinating to make a study of nature's trees and visualise bonsai shapes'. However, not all trees in nature have enough visual impact to inspire a new style. When standing in front of a 90-metre-tall, 2 000-year-old Redwood tree, with a columnar trunk devoid of branches, the immense height of the tree would immediately lead one to categorise its style as 'formal upright'.

When John Naka was standing in front of a huge baobab tree, with its barrel-like trunk approximately 16 metres in diameter and well over 3 000 years old, he said that he felt like a tiny piece of dust lying on a mountain. Today we have the baobab style as a true African style.

Although bonsai originated in China, the Japanese have had the biggest influence on the bonsai concept and philosophy as we know it today. Likewise, Western bonsai growers, especially the Americans, have been influenced by their environment and culture to develop a new way of expressing this oriental art form. Similarly, the author created new indigenous African styles like the baobab, the Pierneef, the flat top, the bushveld, the wild fig and others, as the climate and tree shapes in Africa are totally different to those found in the Northern Hemisphere.

A baobab tree in nature.

A redwood tree in Sequoia National Park.

32

Classification of bonsai styles

Basic styles

Despite a multitude of bonsai styles, only five main basic styles form the back bone of all the styles.

- Formal upright or Chokkan style
- Informal upright or Moyo-gi style
- Slanting or Shakan style
- Semi-cascade or Han-kengai style
- Full cascade or Kengai style

These styles are identified by the angle at which each tree trunk slants towards the horizontal line.

Index of bonsai styles

The following index summarises the different bonsai styles, their main characteristics, and the Japanese equivalent, where applicable.

Upright styles		
Style	**Characteristics**	**Japanese equivalent**
Baobab (p. 185)	Barrel trunk	African style
Broom (p. 79)	Broom shape	Hoki-zukuri
Bushveld or natural form (p. 200)	Natural shape	Shizen-zukuri
Candle flame (p. 83)	Candle-flame shape	Rosoku-zukuri
Coiled, spiral or twisted (p. 101)	Spiral trunk	Nejikan
Flat top (p. 196)	Funnel-shaped branch structure	African style
Formal upright or straight trunk (p. 41)	Straight formal trunk	Chokkan
Gnarled (p. 91)	Gnarled trunk	Bankan
Group plantings (p. 160)	Trees suggesting forests	Yose-uye
Hollow trunk (p. 96)	Hollowed trunk	Sabakan / Saba-miki
Informal upright (p. 49)	Informal trunk line	Moyo-gi
Knobby trunk	Knobby trunk	Kobukan
Literati (p. 130)	Free form	Bunjin
Pierneef (p. 190)	Umbrella crown	African style
Pine tree (p. 85)	Pine-tree shape	Matsu-zukuri
Slanting (p. 58)	Slanted trunk line	Shakan
Strangler (p. 94)	Tree with aerial roots which eventually strangle the host tree	–
Struck-by-lightning (p. 92)	Bark peeled from the trunk to form jins and shari's	Kaminari
Willow or weeping (p. 87)	Hanging branches	Shidare-zukuri
Wild fig (p. 203)	Umbrella-shaped crown	Kasa-zukuri

Tree shapes

Style	Characteristics	Japanese equivalent
Baobab (p. 185)	Barrel trunk	African style
Broom (p. 79)	Broom shape	Hoki-zukuri
Candle flame (p. 83)	Candle-flame shape	Rosoku-zukuri
Cedar tree (p. 41)	Triangular shape	Chokkan
Flat top (p. 196)	Funnel shape	African style
Pierneef (p. 190)	Umbrella shape	Kasa-zukuri
Pine tree (p. 85)	Pine-tree shape	Matsu-zukuri
Wild fig (p. 203)	Umbrella shape	Kasa-zukuri
Willow (p. 87)	Weeping form	Shidare-zukuri

Multiple trunks developed from a single root system

Style	Characteristics	Japanese equivalent
Fallen tree (p. 118)	A fallen tree of which the branches grow upwards	Ikadabuki
Raft (p. 118)	Shoots sprouting from surface roots	Netsuranari
Sprout (p. 125)	Multiple trunks with one root base	Kabudachi
Turtle-back or stump (p. 123)	Swollen base like the shell of a tortoise	Korabuki

Trees sharing a single root system

Style	Characteristics	Japanese equivalent
Double-trunk (p. 113)	Two trunks sharing the same root system	Sokan
Triple-trunk (p. 156)	Three trunks sharing the same root system	Sankan
Five-trunk	Five trunks sharing the same root system	Gokan
Seven-trunk	Seven trunks sharing the same root system	Nanakan
Nine-trunk	Nine trunks sharing the same root system	Kyukan

Styles suggesting nature

Style	Characteristics	Japanese equivalent
Group plantings (p. 160)	Simulating forests or groves of trees	Yose-uye
Rock-clinging (p. 108)	Trees growing in crevices in rocks	Ishi-zuke
Root-over-rock (p. 104)	Roots growing over rocks	Seki-jo-ju
Struck-by-lightning (p. 92)	Struck by lightning	Kaminari
Split trunk (p. 89)	Trunk splits into two	Sogu-ki
Windswept (p. 138)	Windswept	Fuki-nagashi
Strangler (p. 94)	Roots that strangle the host tree	–

Avant-garde bonsai styles

Style	Characteristics	Japanese equivalent
Driftwood (p. 146)	Sculpturing of dead wood	Shari-miki
Literati or free form (p. 130)	Free and artistically formed trees	Bunjin
Windswept (p. 138)	Windswept	Fuki-nagashi

Trees with extraordinary branch structures

Style	Characteristics	Japanese equivalent
Elbow (p. 205)	Wide-spreading branches start to root when they touch the ground. Also known as the Wonderboom style	African style
Elongated branch (p. 98)	The main branch is over-developed and straggles to one side	Tatami-mat / Goza-kake
Octopus (p. 180)	Dramatic branch structures	Tako-zukuri
Willow (p. 87)	Hanging branches	Shidare-zukuri

Trees with inclined trunks

Style	Characteristics	Japanese equivalent
Full cascade (p. 67)	Trunk cascades over the edge of a cliff	Kengai
Semi-cascade (p. 67)	Trunk cascades half-way over the edge of a cliff	Han-kengai
Slanting (p. 58)	Slanted trunk	Shakan
Windswept (p. 138)	Windswept	Fuki-nagashi

Cascading styles

Style	Characteristics	Japanese equivalent
Full cascade (p. 67)	Trunk cascades over the edge of a cliff	Kengai
Semi-cascade (p. 67)	Trunk cascades halfway over the edge of a cliff	Han-kengai

Dramatic tree styles

Style	Characteristics	Japanese equivalent
Baobab (p. 185)	Barrel trunk	African style
Driftwood (p. 146)	Sculpturing of dead wood	Shari-miki
Exposed roots (p. 177)	Exposed roots form the focal point of the style	Ne-agari
Gnarled (p. 91)	Gnarled trunk	Bankan
Hollow trunk (p. 96)	Hollowed trunk	Sabakan / Saba-miki
Knobby trunk	Knobby trunk	Kobukan
Octopus (p. 180)	Dramatic branch structure	Tako-zukuri
Peeled bark	Bark peeled from trunk	Sharikan
Struck-by-lightning (p. 92)	Bark peeled from the trunk to form jins and shari's	Kaminari

Trees associated with rocks

Style	Characteristics	Japanese equivalent
Rock clinging (p. 108)	Trees growing in crevices in rocks	Ishi-zuke
Root-over-rock (p. 104)	Roots growing over a rock into the soil	Seki-jo-ju

Group plantings comprising more than two separate trees

Style	Characteristics	Japanese equivalent
Twin-tree (p. 151)	Two trees	Soju
Triple-tree (p. 156)	Three trees	Samon-yose
Five-tree	Five trees	Gohan-yose
Seven-tree	Seven trees	Nanakan-yose
Nine-tree	Nine trees	Kyuhan-yose
Multiple group (p. 160)	More than eleven trees	Yose-uye
Cone or fist arrangement	Sprouts from a fallen cone	Tsukomi-yose / Yama-yori

Chinese-originated styles

Style	Characteristics	Japanese equivalent
Horai (p. 175)	Trunks and branches are strangely curved and twisted	Horai
Literati or free form (p. 130)	An artistic Chinese style dating back to the year 206 AC	Bunjin
Octopus (p. 180)	Branches curve like the tentacles of an octopus	Tako-zukuri
Penjin (p. 170)	Included in this style are several Chinese art forms such as Chinese landscape paintings, garden works of art, pruning of single trees, as well as the creation of miniature landscapes.	Penjin
Plaited or entwined trunk (p. 182)	Trunks (especially vines) are cloned together to form a trunk	Pien-tshu / Karame-miki

Trees with exposed roots

Style	Characteristics	Japanese equivalent
Aerial roots	Aerial roots that hang from the main branches	–
Buttressed root	Buttressed roots that grow flat and upright round the tree	–
Exposed roots 177	Exposed roots form the focal point of this style	Ne-agari
Plaited or twisted root	Roots plaited to form a trunk	–
Strangler roots (p. 94)	Roots that strangle the host tree	–

African-originated styles

Style	Characteristics	Japanese equivalent
Baobab (p. 185)	Tree with a remarkable girth	–
Bushveld or natural form (p. 200)	Naturally formed trees found in the Savanna Bushveld	–
Elbow or Wonderboom shape (p. 205)	Wide-spreading branches start to root when they touch the ground	–
Flat top (p. 196)	Funnel-shaped trees with flat crowns	–
Pierneef (p. 190)	Umbrella-shaped crowns	–
Wild fig (p. 203)	Wide-spreading umbrella-shaped crowns with short trunks	–

Basic styles

Formal upright or straight trunk style – Chokkan

Informal upright style – Moyo-gi or Tachiki

Slanting style – Shakan

Cascade style – Kengai

Pinus pentaphylla var. *himekomatsu*:
For the novice the slightly curved trunk
would possibly disqualify this as a
formal upright style. The tree,
however, is an excellent example
of a natural upright style with
shari. Note the first branch is
at the back. Branches of
the multiple-bud five-
needle pine were grafted
on the original trunk to
create this outstanding
tree – one of the
late Mr Iwasaki's
masterpieces.
Height 85 cm.

Formal upright or straight trunk style – Chokkan

There is an old saying in the bonsai world that says:
'creating a bonsai begins with the formal upright and ends with the formal upright'.

When one thinks of upright trees, one thinks of pines, cedars and conifers. Although these magnificent trees form the basis of the formal upright style, a few deciduous trees, such as the baobab with its impressive thick trunk and the traditional broom, could also be classified under this style. These two styles, despite their formal trunks, however are not examples of the classical Chokkan style.

As the style dictates, the trunk must be straight and none, or very little, movement is allowed in the trunk line. The formal upright style has originated in the Northern Hemisphere where these beautiful masterpieces are found in nature. The most impressive formal upright trees that I know of are, without a doubt, the giant redwoods (*Sequoia gigantea*) growing in the Yosemite Park in California. These giants pierce the air up to 90 metres (300 ft), and are regarded as the tallest trees on earth.

In Europe we find the majestic cedars of the Lebanon and in Asia the Himalayan cedars. These trees are traditionally formed in the triangular shape, as this is their normal growing pattern in nature. In Japan we have the white, black and red pines, as well as the beautiful ezo spruce (*Picea* species), and cryptomerias. In South Africa the impressive *Podocarpus* species, or yellowwood trees, are found in forest areas around the country. These are remnants of the forest that covered most of Southern Africa three hundred thousand years ago.

It is necessary for beginners to learn the basic structure and shape of the formal upright style before moving on to other styles. Once the beginner has mastered the basics of this style, he or she can apply the same basic principles to most other styles.

This *Buddleja saligna* tree was collected by the author in 1990 and designed into this elegant formal upright style. Height 120 cm.

41

Guidelines for creating a formal upright style

Root base

Surface roots should spread out evenly round the trunk, as they should not grow straight towards the front.

The roots should spread out evenly round the trunk to create an impression of stability.
Avoid an octopus-like root system as it will mar the beauty of the tree. To correct this problem, flatten out the roots if at all possible, and pin them down with wires.

Trunk shape

The straight trunk is the dominant feature of the style, and should create a feeling of strength and stability. None or very little movement is allowed in the trunk line. Movement is created by the placement of the branches.

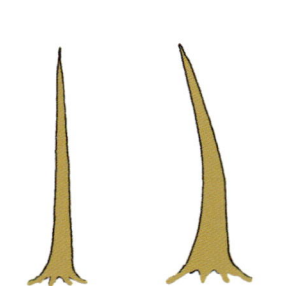

The trunk tapers from the base to the apex, and the apex may lean slightly to the front.

A heavy trunk gives a feeling of strength and dominance.

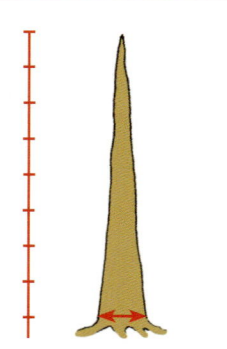

The height of the tree is approximately six to eight times the diameter of the trunk.

Branch placement

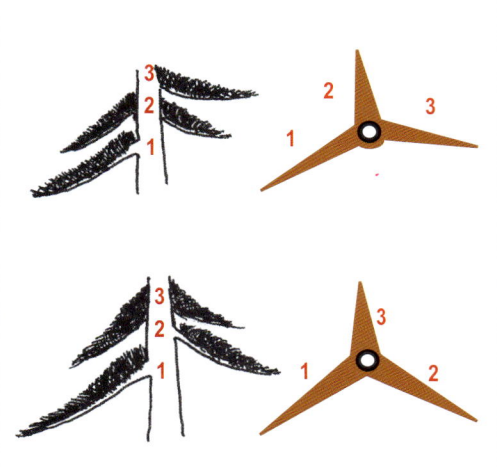

Viewed from above, the branches should give the impression of being grouped in layers of three. Branches should not be placed directly above one another to allow for as much sunlight as possible.

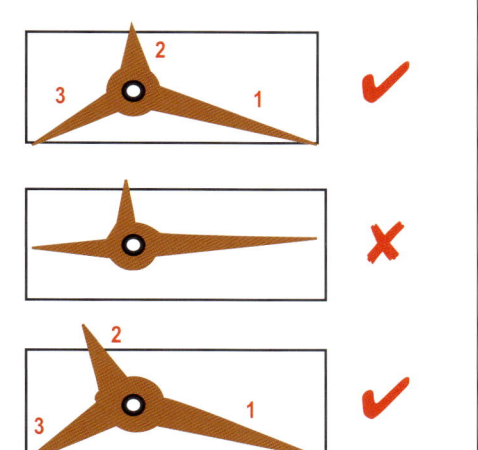

The number one branch usually fills the biggest portion of the container. The number one and number three branches must be trained to grow diagonally in the container otherwise the composition will look flat and unattractive. The three main branches point towards the corners of the pot.

Points to remember when creating a formal upright style

- Place the number one branch to the left or to the right, as it is the longest and the most prominent branch in the composition.

- Place the number one branch at a point one-third to one-half of the height of the tree. The height can, however, vary according to personal taste or the number of branches available.

- Place the number three branch opposite the number one branch. This branch is the second most important branch in the composition.

- The back branch (number two) must never be the first (number one) branch.

- Keep the front and back branches short.

- Train the branches in the form of a spiral staircase round the trunk.

- All the branches are of different lengths and are getting shorter towards the apex.

- Allow the branches to grow denser towards the apex.

- Do not place branches directly opposite one another.

- All branches must have the same movement in order to complement the style.

- Branches are usually wider near the base and taper towards the apex.

Variations on the upright style

Young formal upright tree

Note that the main branches grow horizontally but the branches above them grow progressively more upwards as they approach the apex.

Old formal upright tree

The branches are forced downwards due to the weight of snow or the length of the branches.

Double trunk formal upright

The double trunk or Sokan share the same root base and the two trunks form a harmonious unit. Formal upright trees are normally planted in rectangular containers as they complement the formal style.

Thin trunk tree

Keep the branches short to emphasise the thin trunk. Because of the elegant appearance of the thin trunk, the tree could therefore also be trained into the literati or free style.

Triple trunk formal upright

This magnificent deodar tree stands in front of the well-known Melrose House in Pretoria. It is an excellent example of a multiple trunk. A deep rectangular container gives stability to the composition.

Hollow trunk formal upright

Hollow trunks often occur in nature and here it heightens the dramatic effect of this formal upright tree. A deep rectangular container with inclined corners emphasises the dramatic effect of the tree.

Formal upright tree with jins and shari

The bark has been partially peeled off to give the effect of a tree suffering harsh conditions. A deep oval container is selected to capture the movement created by the jins.

Umbrella crown

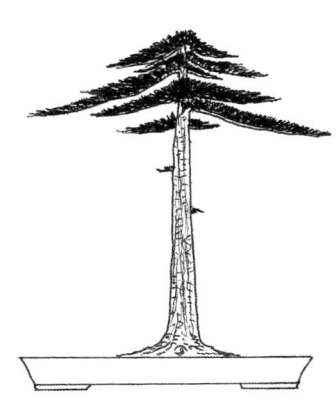

Branches growing towards the apex are kept close together like an umbrella. This style suggests a tree growing at high altitudes. The tree is placed on the right side of the container to allow for the movement of the third main branch on the left. A shallow rectangular container with sharp corners captures the mood of the wide crown.

Closed umbrella style

Branches are trained straight down like a folded umbrella to create this elegant effect. The rectangular container without an outer lip, rounds off the composition.

Wide branches

Wide branches normally complement a short and thick trunk. A deep sturdy container adds to the feeling of strength and stability.

Tree struck by lightning

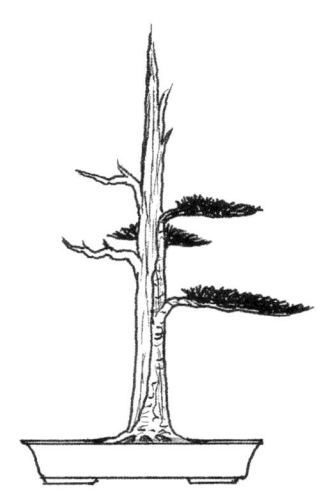

The trunk and apex are scarred to depict a dead tree. Keep the remaining branches sparse to portray the effects of a harsh environment. An oval container, the length of which is approximately half the height of the trunk, emphasises the height of the tree.

The effect of strong winds

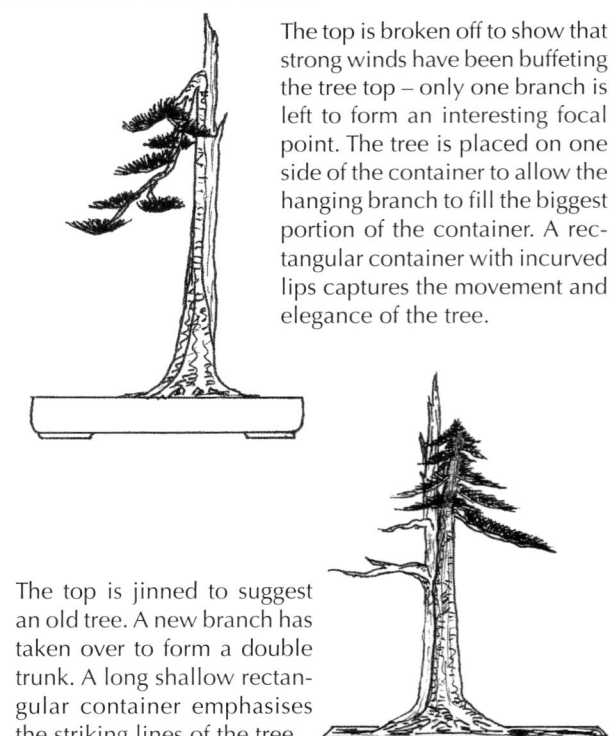

The top is broken off to show that strong winds have been buffeting the tree top – only one branch is left to form an interesting focal point. The tree is placed on one side of the container to allow the hanging branch to fill the biggest portion of the container. A rectangular container with incurved lips captures the movement and elegance of the tree.

The top is jinned to suggest an old tree. A new branch has taken over to form a double trunk. A long shallow rectangular container emphasises the striking lines of the tree.

Deciduous trees grown in a formal upright manner

Deciduous conifers

The bald or swamp cypress (*Taxodium distichum*) and the European larch (*Larix decidua*) are the only true deciduous conifer species which can be trained into the formal upright style. An oval container is selected to highlight the feminine mood of the tree.

Baobab shape

Although the branch structure of the baobab tree is informal, it may be classified as a formal upright style because of its thick and formal trunk. This style is discussed in greater detail under the heading *Baobab style* on page 185.

Broom shape

The single formal upright trunk tapers towards the apex to form the formal broom style. The *Celtis*, elm, and *Zelkova* species are ideal for this style. This subject will be discussed in greater detail under the heading *Broom style* on page 79.

Candle-flame shape

The candle-flame shape, as found in nature among the ginkgo's, liquidambars, alders, and beech species, may be classified as a formal upright style. This style is discussed in greater detail under the heading *Candle-flame style* on page 83.

Containers

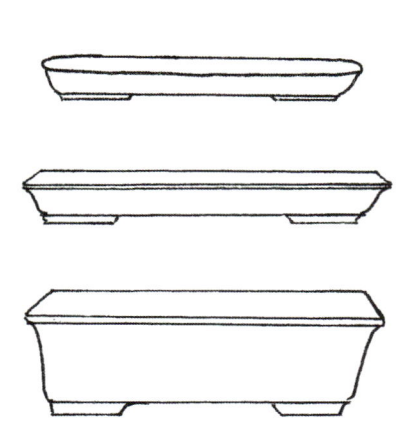

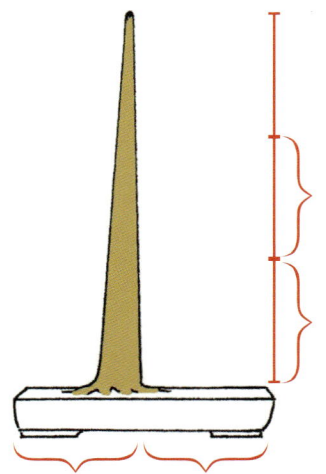

Oval and rectangular containers complement most of the formal styles. Tall, thin trunks look elegant in shallow containers. Thick trunks need deep containers to heighten the effect of stability.

The length of the container is normally equal to two-thirds the height of the tree, while the depth of the container is approximately equal to the diameter of the trunk.

Plant material

Evergreen plant material and, especially, the needle species such as the various pines, cedars, conifers, yews, *Picea*, and *Podocarpus* are regarded as the best material for creating the formal upright style.

The bald or swamp cypress (*Taxodium distichum*) as well as the European larch (*Larix decidua*) are ideal for deciduous plant material.

This swamp cypress by Erika Kohler is a good example of a deciduous tree trained into the formal upright style.

Informal upright style – Moyo-gi or Tachiki

The informal upright style is one of the five basic styles, and is usually popular in most collections.

As the name indicates, the informal upright style is based on an informal trunk and branch structure. The overall shape is triangular; the shape that nature has conferred on most of the conifer species and their seed-bearing cones. Deciduous trees trained in this style have a more rounded crown compared to those of conifers.

The Moyo-gi style is one of the oldest styles that has been created by the early masters; many records exist of these trees.

Many of the present masters make no clear distinction between the pine-tree style, the natural style and the slanting style. They often place these styles in the same category, i.e. the informal upright style.

In his article, 'Informal Upright Style for the Novice', in *International Bonsai* 1983/No. 3, Senikichi Nakatsu writes that the term *informal upright* is used loosely and, in fact, refers to several styles which also include the slanting style. The same 'loose' approach is found by other bonsai masters such as Yuyi Yoshimura in his book, *The Japanese Art of Miniature Tree and Landscape*, under the heading 'Training'.

Although small, this wild olive tree (*Olea europaea* subsp. *africana*) is an excellent example of an informal upright style. The tree was styled by the late Theuns Roos. Height 25 cm.

Guidelines for creating an informal upright style

Roots

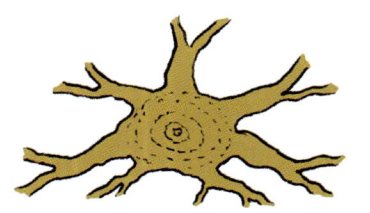

Surface roots should spread evenly around the trunk with the strongest roots to the sides. Make sure that no major roots grow towards the viewer.

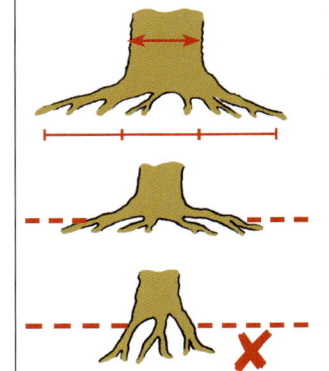

The length of the lateral roots is approximately two to three times the trunk's diameter.

Spread the roots horizontally and not vertically, because the latter arrangement not only looks unnatural but also lacks stability.

Trunk line

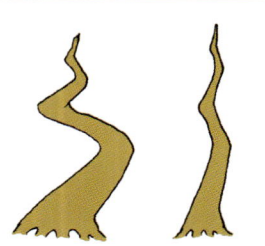

To display the movement of the trunk, choose the side that shows off the trunk movement at its best. The trunk line may curve either sharply or gently.

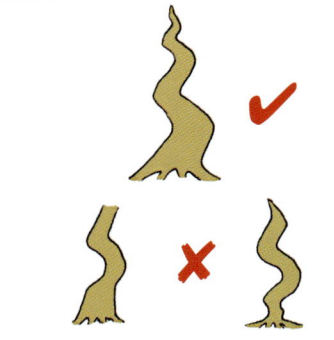

The trunk tapers from the base to the apex. Avoid tree trunks that do not taper, or that taper from the apex to the base, called reverse taper.

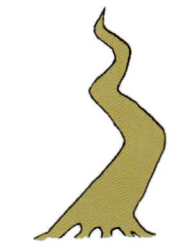

The trunk slopes upwards from the base to the first branch. Thereafter the distances decrease between the bends in the trunk.

When viewed from the front, the major bends should be on both the left and right sides of the trunk. In other words, the trunk must not bend forwards or backwards, otherwise the bends will be invisible to the viewer.

The apex leans slightly towards the viewer at an angle of approximately five degrees. This bowing position is not in humble adoration of its creator, but rather to enhance the optical illusion of a large tree looking down onto you.

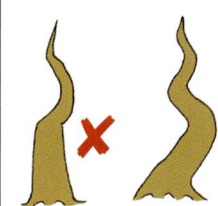

The trunk should not grow vertically upwards, but it should rather slant slightly to the right or the left.

Terminal line

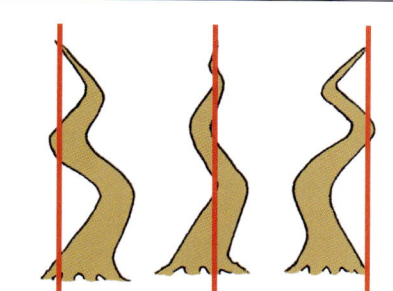

The terminal line tends towards the vertical from the apex to the base. Do not apply this rule too rigidly, as the terminal line could lean a few degrees to either side. Normally the upper trunk should not slope more than fifteen degrees, otherwise the style could be classified as a slanting style.

The distance between curves in the trunk becomes progressively shorter towards the apex. For instance, if the distance between the root base and the first curve were approximately sixteen centimetres, the distance between the following curves would decrease progressively in the following order: eight, four, two and one (regard dimensions as a guideline only).

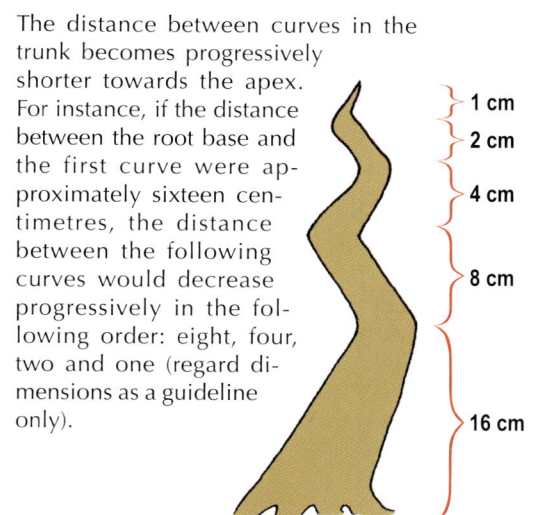

1 cm
2 cm
4 cm
8 cm
16 cm

Branch placement

Main branches must grow from the outside of curves but make sure that no heavy branches point directly towards the viewer. Use the traditional staircase branch placement, i.e. left, back, right and front, towards the top of the tree. No hard and fast rules apply. Just make sure that no branches are placed on top of each other.

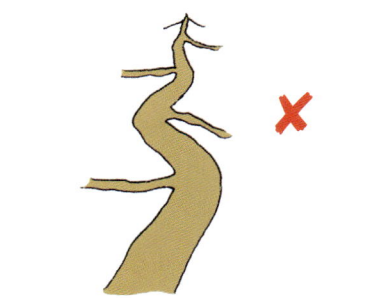

Ensure that no branches grow from the inside of curves, or on the straight portion between curves, as an unnatural and unattractive appearance will be the result.

The first branch (or the number one branch) is usually the strongest and longest, and should be positioned at approximately one-third to half the length of the trunk. Do not apply this rule too rigidly, as branch placement is dependent on the plant material or the mood that the artist intends to capture.

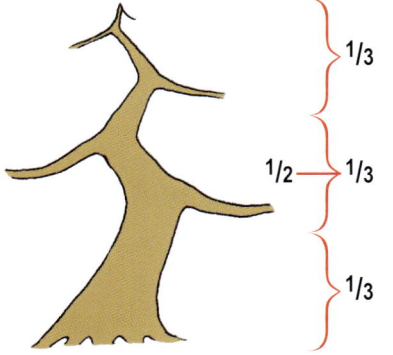

1/3
1/2 — 1/3
1/3

Should a major branch not exist, choose another branch higher up on the trunk. This placement could be an interesting focal point, depending on the type of material available.

Reposition a branch that grows from a wrong point on the trunk, by wiring it upwards or downwards to achieve the required effect.

Remember that branch placement becomes closer towards the apex.

Branch angle

A particular effect is achieved by placing the branches at a certain angle, as shown in the following sketches.

An old tree: Branches of old trees normally droop sharply. To simulate this effect, simply bend the branches downwards.

A tree in its prime: The branches of a tree in its prime usually stretch out horizontally, radiating a feeling of strength and stability.

A young tree: A young tree is normally a vigorous grower, with the result that the lateral branches tend to grow upwards in search of sunlight.

Number of branches

The number of branches depends on the length of the trunk, as shown in the following sketches.

A short trunk should not have too many branches. Rather concentrate on fewer branches, which would, undoubtedly, produce a dramatic end result.

A long trunk should have more branches. A three-branch grouping could be followed, but do not adhere to this rule too rigidly, as the available plant material always plays a major role in the selection of branches.

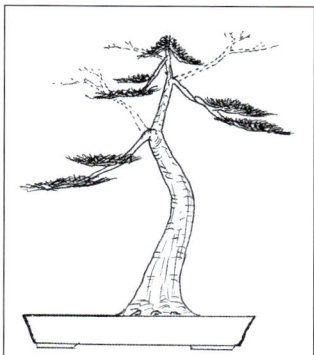

Negative space between the branches could be filled quite easily by bending branches downwards.

Secondary branches

Secondary branches should follow the same movement as the primary branch.

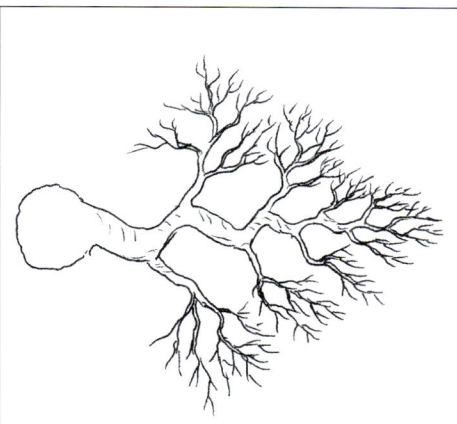

Top view: Viewed from above, branches should form a zigzag pattern. Note that the secondary branches also grow from the outside of curves. The silhouette line is pear-shaped or triangular, and the widest side is closer to the trunk.

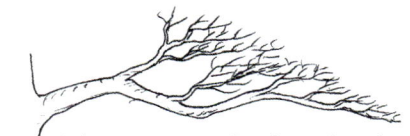

Side view: Secondary branches slant at an angle of approximately forty-five degrees, and taper towards the end of the branch. These branches normally provide the basis for twiggy growth and foliage. The silhouette line tapers towards the tip, and has a triangular or round shape.

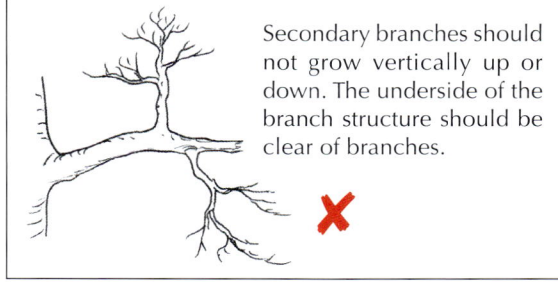

Secondary branches should not grow vertically up or down. The underside of the branch structure should be clear of branches.

Silhouette line

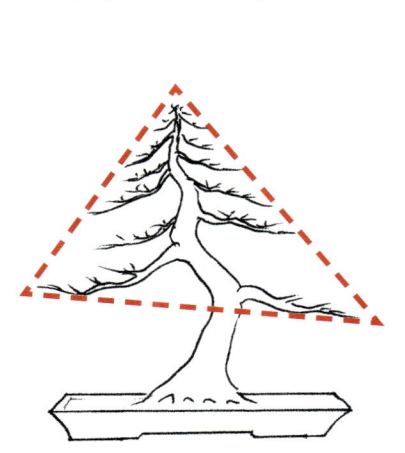

An overall triangular silhouette line is recommended for conifers, while a more rounded one is recommended for deciduous trees and old conifers.

An asymmetrical silhouette line creates an illusion of movement and balance.

A symmetrical silhouette line lacks movement and appears static and uninteresting.

Famous trees in the Moyo-gi style

The famous ezo spruce, which belongs to the Emperor of Japan, is shown in the sketch. The jinned portion of the trunk adds to the character of the tree. The first branch cascades downwards to form an interesting feature. The trunk's movement is emphasised by the inclined lines of the container.

The tall trunk of this Moyo-gi style pine tree is balanced by the cascading primary branch. The tree generates a feeling of movement and elegance, which is heightened by the rounded lines of the container, and which is in sharp contrast to the lines of the pot's outer lip.

An illusion of rhythm and movement is created by the elegant trunk line and the bending down of the branches. A deep oval container is selected to highlight the movement of the trunk.

Despite the heavy trunk of this impressive tree, an illusion of movement is created by the foliage mass that is growing close to the trunk. The sharp outer lip and the step-like legs of the rectangular container emphasise the airy feeling exuded by this tree.

Although the lower portion of the trunk slants slightly, the apical portion of the trunk still forms a vertical line downwards to the base of the tree. The jinned lower trunk gives further movement to the tree. A deep rectangular container without an outer lip, balances the large trunk and upper portion of the tree, and gives stability to the composition.

A deep oval container with a wide outer lip is selected for this majestic Moyo-gi style pine tree. The upper trunk forms the focal point. The sharp curve is balanced by drooping branches and a rounded apex, which complement the circular movement of the tree and the container.

The bowl-shaped container emphasises the slender trunk line of this Moyo-gi style tree. To indicate the front of the tree, the legs of the container are placed on the sides facing the viewer.

This compact tree in the Moyo-gi style is planted in a deep sturdy container with rounded sides, to match the form of the tree. The square-cut legs contribute to the effect of strength and stability.

The exaggerated curvature of the trunk line is balanced by the elongated branch on the left. This branch adds to the dramatic effect created by this interesting arrangement. A deep four-sided container contrasts well with the movement of the tree.

Deciduous trees in the Moyo-gi style

The strong developed roots are the focal point of this fully grown maple tree. A deep oval container emphasises the movement captured in the tree's structure. *Celtis*, elm, hornbeam and other deciduous species can be successfully trained into the Moyo-gi style.

This is a young maple tree, planted in a shallow light-coloured oval container. The beige-coloured container harmonises well with the pale-coloured trunk. Most deciduous trees show off very well in light-coloured containers, especially in autumn and winter.

Fruit-bearing and flowering trees

Fruit-bearing trees, such as the cotoneaster, persimmon, pyracantha and others, are attractive material to develop into the Moyo-gi style. Flowering plants such as the azalea, bougainvillaea and jasmine, are also ideal plants for this style. The soft lines of the flower-shaped pot give a feminine touch to this beautiful tree.

A delicate, feminine feeling is displayed by this mountain maple (*Acer palmatum* var. *matsumurae*) bursting into its spring foliage. The tree belonged to the late Mr Iwasaki. Height 65 cm.

Containers

Depth of the container

The depth of the container is normally equal to the diameter, or even twice the diameter, of the trunk. However, in cold or very hot climates it is better to use deeper containers. South African indigenous plants thrive in deeper containers.

Positioning by visual weight

To create an impression of movement, position the side of the tree with the greatest visual weight close to one side of the container, as eye movement will then normally flow towards the open side of the container.

Length of the container

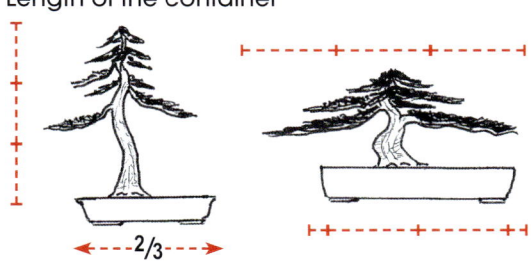

The length of the container is approximately two-thirds the height or the width of the tree; whichever is the major dimension.

Tree placement in the container

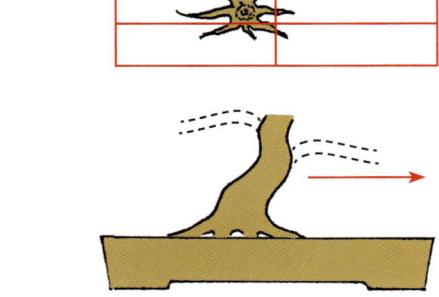

Position the tree trunk just off-centre and towards the back of the container. Make sure that the trunk leans towards the largest area of the container.

Container colour

The colour of the container should contrast or harmonise with the colour of the foliage, flowers or berries. Therefore, plant evergreen trees in grey, brown or dark red terracotta containers, and trees with yellow, orange, red or pink berries or flowers in light or dark blue or grey containers.

Container shape

Normally, equal-sided rectangular containers are used for evergreen trees, because the emphasis here is on trunk movement. On the other hand, deciduous trees look best in oval containers, because of the natural movement of their trunks and branches. For example, use an oval container when the emphasis is on branch movement.

Plant material

In most cases any plant material may be used for the informal upright style, if the leaves are small. Trees with very large leaves such as frangipani, loquat and eucalyptus should be avoided. Most of the conifers, *Olea*, *Buddleja* and *Ficus* species, and other evergreens, are well suited to the style. Deciduous species such as maple, elm, *Celtis* and hornbeam are excellent plant material for this style. The bald or swamp cypress (*Taxodium distichum*) is also ideal.

57

Slanting style – Shakan

The Shakan or slanting style is one of the five basic styles. This pleasing style is found in most collections around the world.

Trees in the slanting styles often occur in nature. The slanting of a tree may be induced by strong winds, landslides or competition for light, hence these trees are often found along windy shores and mountain sides and along ponds or on riverbanks.

Trees grown in this style should give an impression of movement and also radiate strength and endurance. Furthermore, as this style is determined by the lean of the trunk, the composition should always exude a feeling of balance and stability.

Deborah Korreshoff sums it up very well when she states that: 'Slanting style designs are often very active in feeling due to the many tensions involved in their form, and movement may be frozen in space with delicacy and balance.'

Buddleja saligna collected by the late Louis Nel and styled by Roy Nagatoshi. Height 85 cm.

Guidelines for creating a slanting style

Roots

Surface roots play an important role in supporting the leaning trunk.

Roots should spread out horizontally to strengthen the illusion of stability needed for the style. The roots opposite the trunk's lean should be strong and well developed in order to anchor the tree. The strong roots underneath the slant usually have a buttressed appearance owing to compressive forces present in the composition.

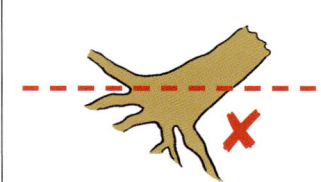

Take care not to:
- plant the tree at a slanting angle
- place the roots opposite the slant in an upright position
- bury the rest of the roots underneath the slant of the tree.

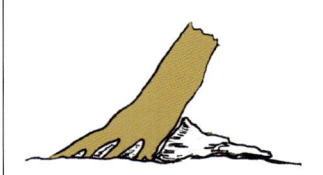

If the root development is only on one side, the strongest root should be opposite the trunk's lean. Adjust the side without roots by using a matching coloured stone as a replacement for the lack of roots.

Slanting positions of the trunk

The Shakan style has three slanting positions, namely:
- a moderate slant (Sho-shakan), which is between 60 and 75 degrees
- a medium slant (Hu-shakan), which is between 45 to 60 degrees
- an extreme slant (Dai-shakan), which is between 30 to 45 degrees.

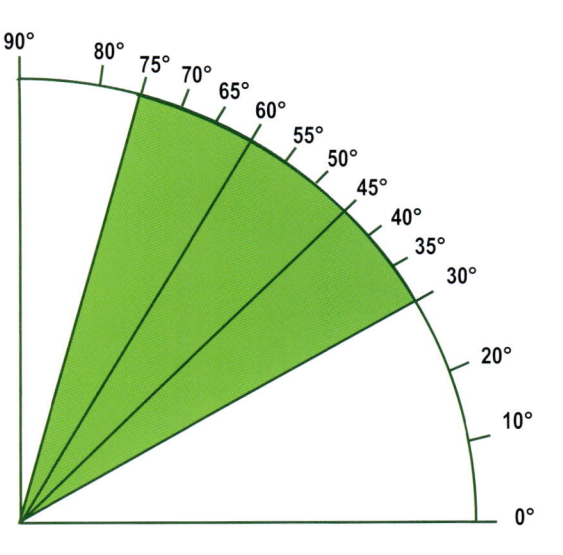

Trunk line

We can distinguish between a formal and informal trunk line.

Formal trunk line

A formal upright tree could develop into a slanting style after, for instance, a landslide or heavy rains followed by strong winds, etc., which could force a tree to lean to one side.

Informal trunk line

The informal slanting style has a naturally curved trunk. It is therefore far easier to create an illusion of stability in the trunk line of an informal slanting tree than in the trunk line of a formal slanting tree. Informal Shakans are usually found in most collections.

Trunk position

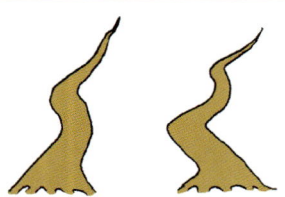

The lower trunk always grows upwards at an angle of roughly 45 degrees. The trunk on the right slants first towards the left before it slants to the right to form an interesting variation.

Traditional slanting style

The primary or second branch, slants away from the trunk's lean at an angle of approximately 25 degrees. Branches are placed in such a manner as to resemble the outstretched arms of a trapeze artist. Despite the angle of the branches, the tips always re-establish themselves into a horizontal position.
The traditional slanting style is always shaped in the sym-metrical form.

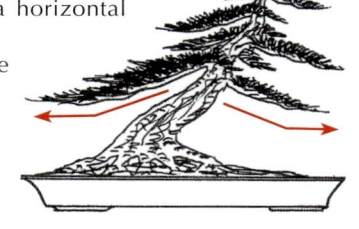

Asymmetrical design

This design emulates a tree that is leaning over a pond in search of sunlight. Movement and rhythm are the prime objectives in this composition. The primary or second branch is the most important one, as it must always be in a horizontal position to balance the trunk's lean.

Reverse apex

The informal slanting trunk line gives grace and rhythm to the creation. To harmonise with the mood of the trunk, the branches follow the same movement.

This *Searsia incisa,* indigenous to South Africa, was collected and styled by the author. Height 40 cm. (The botanical names of trees in the Karee family was recently changed from *Rhus* to *Searsia.*)

Variations on the slanting style

Double-trunk slanting style – Sokan

The form of the major trunk is asymmetrical; the primary branch stretches out over an imaginary pond or cliff; while the minor trunk is in the traditional slanting position. A deep rectangular container helps to increase the effect of stability.

The major tree follows the traditional design, and it is placed above the minor tree in a protective position. The trunk lines are in harmony. They should never cross each other. The primary branch (the number two branch) is placed on the major tree, while the minor branch (the number one branch) is placed on the minor tree.

Triple trunk slanting style – Sankan

The primary tree is placed in the centre; the secondary tree follows the same trunk movement as that of the primary tree; while the minor tree slants sharply downwards to create depth in the composition.
To compensate for the heavy base, use a deep rectangular container.

Branch position

Symmetrical design

The slanting style is traditionally associated with the symmetrical design. The second, or primary branch is the most important one because it depicts the mood of the tree.

The branches on the leaning side tend to grow more horizontally, while those on the opposite side tend to slant downwards. The branches on the leaning side are usually shorter than those on the opposite side.

Asymmetrical design

The asymmetrical design has more movement. The tree in the sketch below, for instance, simulates one growing on a river bank; leaning over the water in search of light. The second or primary branch stretches out horizontally over the water. The branches on the opposite side of the trunk are short and, to balance the composition, they slant sharply downwards.

If the primary branch is positioned high up on the trunk, bend it sharply downwards to fill the large negative space between the branch and the soil level so as to ensure a balanced look. Also bend the branches above the primary branch downwards so that they follow the movement of the primary branch. Spread out the tips of the branches horizontally to stabilise the creation.

If the trunk line bends sharply in the opposite direction, the primary branch should stretch out horizontally. The apex should swing to the right so as to follow the movement of the lower trunk line.

If the trunk line has soft curves and the apex is moving in the same direction as the lower trunk line, the branches could be brought downwards to create movement as well as to harmonise with the flow of the trunk.

Branch positions according to the degree of the trunk's slant

It is interesting to note that the various positions of the primary branch in a manner correspond with the degree of the trunk's slant. The primary branch on a trunk with a moderate slant tends to be symmetrical. However, the more the tree leans to one side, the more the primary branch spreads out to balance itself. Hence the design becomes asymmetrical.

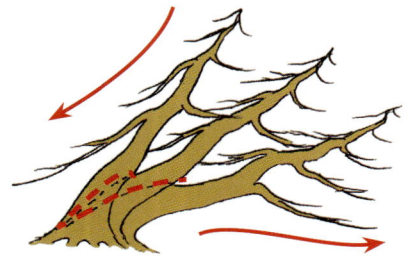

The degree of the trunk's slant does not have a dramatic effect on branch placement, as the branches on the leaning side still tend to stretch out horizontally, while the branches opposite the slant have the same downward angle. Despite the trunk's angle, the branches always re-establish themselves in order to keep their balance.

This *Senegalia galpinii* is a fine example of a slanting Pierneef style. Styled by the author. Height 85 cm. (The botanical name of South African thorn trees was recently changed from *Acacia* to *Senegalia* and *Vachellia*.) The photograph was taken by Sjoerd Knibbeler and Rob Wetzer, two young talented photographers from Amsterdam, the Netherlands.

Terminal point

The terminal point of a slanting style must never be directly above the root base, otherwise the design will be classified as an informal upright style.

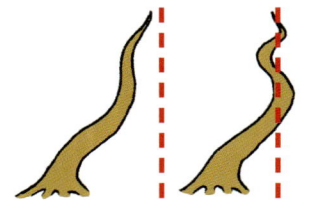

Silhouette line

A rounded apex normally complements the slanting style. In the case of conifers, however, the overall shape of the foliage is triangular, but deciduous trees can have a more rounded crown.

Examples of masterpieces grown in the slanting style

Symmetrical design

The foliage creates a compact triangle which is complemented by the incurved lines of the container. Note that the apex only just extends over the edge of the container to give an impression of movement.

Asymmetrical design

This asymmetrical design has a primary branch that extends over the edge of the container. Although the trunk line is fairly straight, the tree still radiates a feeling of movement. The roots are well spread around the tree, creating an impression of stability. The container has rounded corners in order to place emphasis on the movement of the tree.

A gently slanting design

In this design the trunk slants gently while the branches hang downwards to give an illusion of tranquillity and peace. A deep rectangular container with rounded corners emphasises the soft lines of the tree.

Reverse slant of apical portion

Although the lower portion of the trunk slants to the right, the apical portion swings to the left to form an informal upper portion. A feeling of stability is created by the two lower primary branches which balance the composition. The soft rounded curves of the rectangular container highlight the impression of movement and balance.

Design with apex above the root base

Although the apex is above the root base, the dominant impact is still one of a slanting style. The primary branch swings back against the trunk-flow to balance the interesting trunk line. The broken branch on the trunk's curve accentuates the feeling of movement and rhythm of the tree. The sharp curves of the container also emphasise the slanting angle of the trunk.

Design with primary branch balancing negative space

A soft and gentle effect is achieved in this design. The primary branch balances the negative space on the leaning side, while the branches on the upper portion balance the space on the opposite side. A deep oval container rounds off the composition.

Deciduous trees in the slanting style

Most deciduous trees can be styled into very attractive slanting styles. The trees are most attractive in winter when their branch ramification is best appreciated. Flowers and berries on trees are a bonus, and the various seasonal moods add to the attractiveness of the trees. The apexes of deciduous trees are usually broader than those of the evergreens.

An old deciduous tree in the extreme slanting style

An interesting aspect of this tree is that the lower portion of the trunk first slants to the left and then to the right. This radical change in the trunk line adds to the character and beauty of the tree. A deep rectangular container complements the composition.

Branch structure of deciduous trees

The branches of deciduous trees tend to grow more upwards than those of evergreens. The branch line is more horizontal than that of an evergreen tree. The sharp lines of the rectangular container contrast well with the movement of the tree.

Containers

Trees with thick trunks and heavy crowns are usually planted in equally deep oval or rectangular containers, while trees with thin trunks are planted in round containers. Long, narrow, rectangular containers are not recommended as they emphasise the uninteresting parallel lines of the tree trunks.

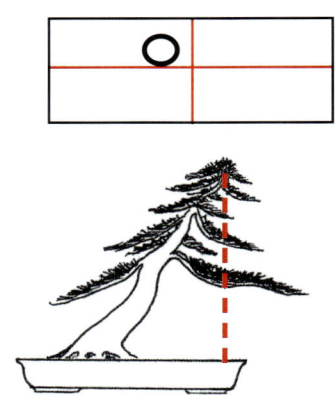

Position the tree just off-centre, towards the back of the container. Make sure that the trunk leans towards the largest open area in the container. The trunk line should not extend too far over the edge of the container.

The sketch shows the wrong way to position a slanting tree in the symmetrical design. The tree should be planted towards the left of the container.

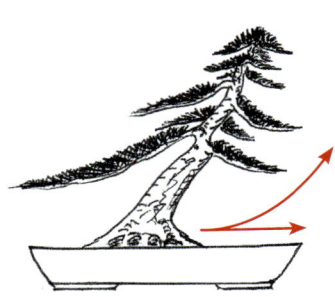

The sketch shows the correct way to position a tree in a container. The slant of the trunk is the deciding factor. The trunk should slant towards the largest open area in the container.

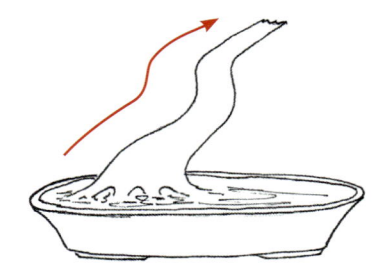

The flow of the trunk usually determines the form of the container. Oval containers are recommended for trees with gently flowing curves in their trunk lines.

Plant material

Almost any plant material can be used for the slanting style, but when evergreen trees are used, make sure that the leaves are small and in proportion to the height and size of the tree.

Cascade style – Kengai

The Japanese word for cascade is *kengai*, which means trees hanging from cliffs. In nature these trees grow against mountainsides, cliffs along seashores, and on precipices.

It often happens that low growing branches die back due to a lack of active sap flow, hence the cascade style demands more from a tree than the upright style.

The cascade style has a charm of its own and can portray many facets of nature, such as cascading waterfalls, mountain winds, steep cliffs, and mountain terrain.

The cascade style is very popular in China. However, the Japanese cascades have a softer appearance compared to the rugged appearance of the Chinese cascades.

Pinus pentaphylla var. *himekomatsu*: This interesting combination of a semi-cascade versus exposed root style is one of the late Mr Iwasaki's favourite trees as it reminds him of wildly grown mountains.

Classification of cascades

Cascades are classified into two categories, namely the semi-cascade and the full cascade.

Semi-cascade (Han-kengai)

The semi-cascade falls midway between the slanting style and the full cascade. The dominant first branch drops at an angle of approximately forty-five degrees. The lower trunk line should not drop below the base of the pot.

Full cascade (Kengai)

The full cascade depicts a tree overhanging a cliff. A variety of styles is found in this group, e.g. the formal, informal, waterfall, windswept, literati, etc. A cascade can be created with or without a crown.

Guidelines for creating a cascade style

Trunk

45°

The trunk slants approximately forty-five degrees to one side.

The trunk should never grow vertically in the container as it looks unnatural.

The first bend in the trunk is always as sharp as possible. Avoid uninteresting half-moon shapes.

Trunk line

Both the semi-cascade and the full cascade can be with or without an upper trunk line. Furthermore, the upper trunk line can be sub-classified into an informal or a slanting trunk line. The branch structures of both these trunk lines follow the same rules that apply to the informal and slanting styles, as discussed in the previous section.

The following sketches illustrate cascades with an upper trunk line.

Informal upper trunk line

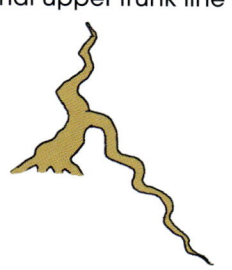

Always select a branch on the outside of a curve and never on the inside of a curve in the trunk line, to form the cascading branch. Furthermore, as the emphasis is on the cascading branch, do not overdevelop the upper trunk line.

Slanting upper trunk line

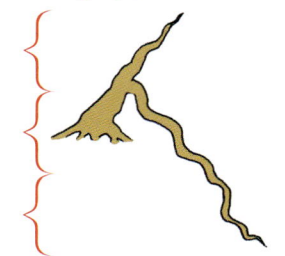

As in the case of the informal upper trunk line, the slanting upper trunk line must also not exceed one-third of the length of the cascading branch.

Note that the cascading branch must not touch the edge of the container.

Roots

The root base needs to be firmly established. The roots opposite the lean of the trunk should give the impression that they are anchoring the tree. The buttress roots underneath the cascading branch are the result of compressive forces acting on the side.

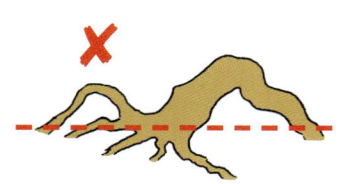

Always remove all upward-growing roots as they look unnatural.

Do not plant the tree too deep in the pot as the main roots should be clearly visible above the edge of the pot.

The basic rule for creating a cascade is to position the tree in the centre of the container, even though the apex of the trunk line will be slightly off-centre because of the slanting position of the main trunk.

69

Branch position

Position of the cascading branch

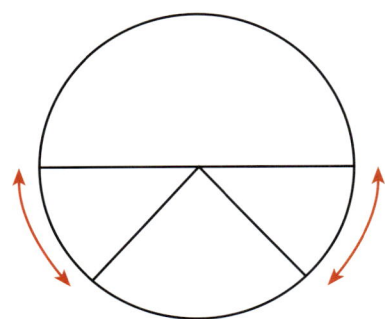

The position from where the trunk should cascade over the edge of a container may be either to the left or to the right in a forward position, when viewed from above.

Branch structure of the semi-cascade

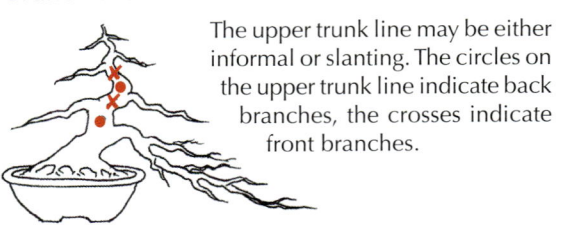

The upper trunk line may be either informal or slanting. The circles on the upper trunk line indicate back branches, the crosses indicate front branches.

Branch structure of the full cascade

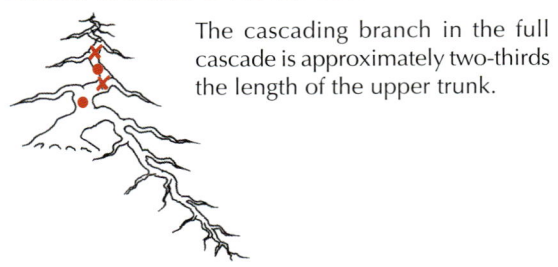

The cascading branch in the full cascade is approximately two-thirds the length of the upper trunk.

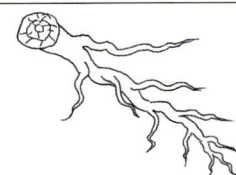

This sketch shows the branch arrangement of the cascading branch from above. The first branch is always a side branch. The branches alternate towards the tip. Front branches are positioned on top of the cascading branch. No undergrowth or back branches are allowed on the cascading branch.

Informal upper trunk line

The first branch on the informal upper trunk line could be a back branch, to give depth to the structure. However, the first branch on the cascading branch is always a side branch. The latter rule applies to both the semi-cascade and the full cascade, including trees with or without an upper trunk line.

Slanting upper trunk line

The same rules that apply to the branch arrangement on the informal upper trunk line apply to the branch arrangement on the slanting upper trunk line. The only difference is that the first branch on the slanting upper trunk line is always a back branch, to create depth. This rule applies only to the upper trunk lines in cascades.

To achieve a good shape, branches must be placed on the outside of a curve. Remove all branches growing underneath the cascading branch and keep top branches short.

Train all secondary branches slightly downwards and tertiary branches slightly upwards, to form a basis for the foliage.

The first branch on the opposite side of the slant gives balance to the slanting trunk. Once the design of the trunk line is established, all branches must follow the same movement.

Train the branches on the cascading branch in the classical 'rule-of-three' arrangement, i.e., sideways, on top and alternately. Note that on the lower arrangement the branches are formed sideways, and the third branch is trained as the top branch. This 'rule-of-three' could be modified should the final structure lack harmony.

Mistakes to avoid

Avoid the following mistakes when creating the cascade style:

Avoid the 'fishbone' arrangement in cascades, as this not only looks artificial and uninteresting but lacks depth and character as well.

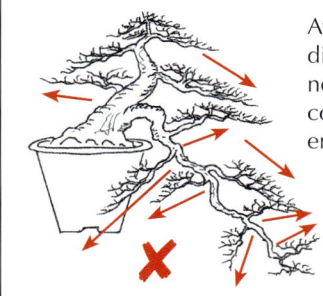

Avoid branches pointing in all directions, as it will distract the normal eye movement and will contribute towards a displeasing end result.

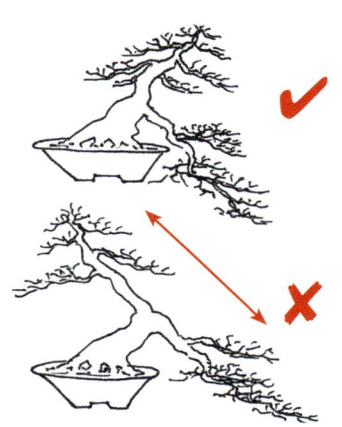

Avoid opposite trunk lines, as they look artificial. Rather train the trunk lines to flow in the same direction.

71

The yellow berries of this full cascade add
to the beauty of this *Pyracantha angustfolia*.
Length 55 cm.

Silhouette line

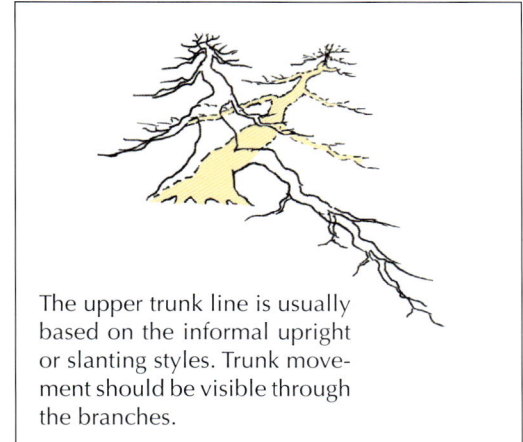

The foliage on the upper trunk and the cascading branch should be equal in mass. This rule applies especially to semi-cascading trees. In the full cascade, however, the foliage mass on the upper portion of the trunk should be less than that on the cascading branch.

The upper trunk line is usually based on the informal upright or slanting styles. Trunk movement should be visible through the branches.

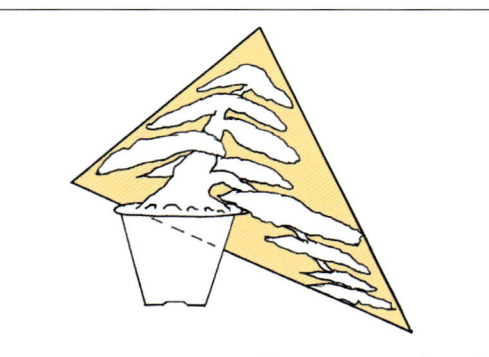

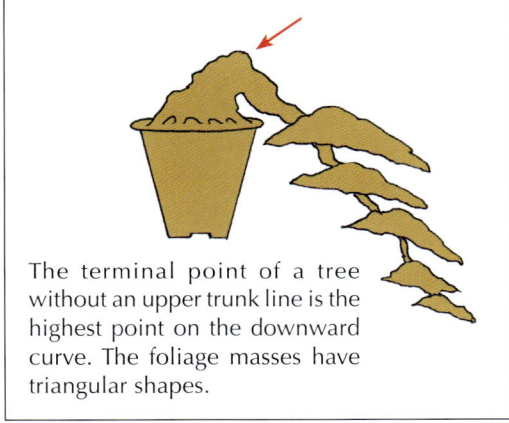

The overall silhouette of the semi-cascade and the full cascade styles is triangular.

The terminal point of a tree without an upper trunk line is the highest point on the downward curve. The foliage masses have triangular shapes.

Cascade styles: cascades with an upper trunk line

Formal cascade

In the formal cascade, the trunk or trunks are fairly straight, to give the style a formal appearance.

Informal cascade

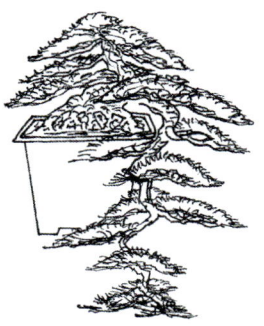

The appearance of the tree is informal; therefore the cascading branch may curve either inwards or outwards.

73

Split trunk cascade

Although the style seems unusual, it happens sometimes in nature that the trunk is split by lightning or by strong winds. The cascading branch is dominant, and the upright trunk is in a supporting position. A deep round or square container may be used to add stability to the composition.

Root-over-rock cascade

The root-over-rock cascade could be either a semi-cascade or a full cascade. Furthermore, it could have an upper trunk line or it could be without a crown. A flat dish-like container may be used, as shown in the sketch. Note that the tip of the cascading branch should not be lower than the soil level in the container.

Twin trunk and triple trunk cascades (Takan-kengai)

The twin trunk and triple trunk cascades, like their upright counterparts, should follow the same trunk movement. The main branch must be stronger and longer than the other two branches. However, the second and third branches are in a minor but complementary position. Use a deep container to stabilise this composition.

Cascade styles: cascades without an upper trunk line

Waterfall cascade (Taki-kengai)

The cascading branches resemble a waterfall. The dense foliage symbolises the mist that is formed by the tumbling waters.

Heavy trunk cascade

A heavy trunk, suitable for a cascade, is not often found in nature or at nurseries. However, when one is fortunate enough to find such a trunk, one should develop it into a heavy trunk cascade. To emphasise the trunk's thickness, keep the branches short. To further emphasise the massiveness of the trunk, and to balance the composition, use a deep round container.

74

Literati cascade

A cascade in the literati style should be elegant with lots of trunk movement. Keep the foliage sparse to emphasise the delicate lines of the style. A tall container with a narrow shape should be used.

Driftwood cascade

A driftwood cascade should create an illusion of a tree struggling for survival against the elements. The top portion is jinned and a side branch cascades downwards. Keep the foliage sparse to emphasise the harsh conditions the tree is experiencing.

Vertical cascade (Dai-kengai)

This bonsai depicts a tree that is drooping almost vertically over the edge of a cliff. This style is best displayed without an upper crown. A tall and narrow-shaped container is recommended for this style.

Gnarled cascade

The emphasis here is on the gnarled cascading trunk. Therefore, keep the foliage compact and dense. The acute angles of the hexagonal container contrast well with the soft curves of the trunk.

Penjin- or Chinese-styled cascade

Here, the emphasis is placed on the dramatic impact of the tree, which has the shape of a dragon striking with flaming tongues. It is typical of Chinese-styled trees to tell a story. A traditional cascade container is recommended.

Exposed roots cascade

The exposed roots style lends itself naturally to the cascade style. These exposed roots form a basis from where the branches cascade downwards. A hexagonal container gives stability to the composition.

Windswept cascade

To capture the effect of winds buffeting the tree, the movement of the cascading branch should be in the same direction the wind blows, therefore the branches should have very little foliage. The thin finger-like jins pointing in the direction the wind blows, accentuate the windswept effect. A tall and narrow-shaped container highlights this phenomenon sometimes seen in nature.

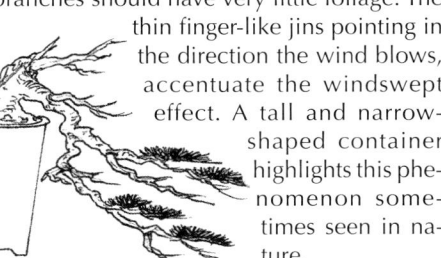

This juniper tree, created by Lynn Theodorou, is a good example of the semi-cascade style.

Containers

Semi-cascades are usually planted in round, hexagonal or square containers. The depth of the container should be three to five times the trunk's diameter.

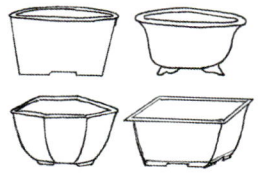

Full cascades are usually planted in deep round or square containers. The depth of the container should be at least half the length of the cascading branch.

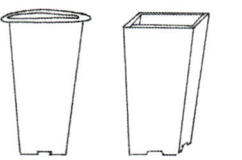

Do not plant a cascade in a shallow container, as the composition would not convey a feeling of depth, namely trees which are cascading naturally down steep cliffs.

The tree and the container should complement each other, i.e. if the tree exudes a powerful feeling, the container should do the same. Delicate trees are usually planted in narrow and deep containers.

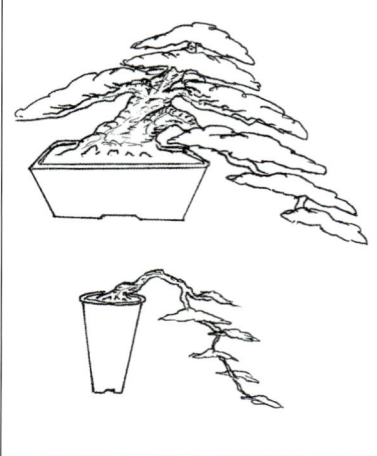

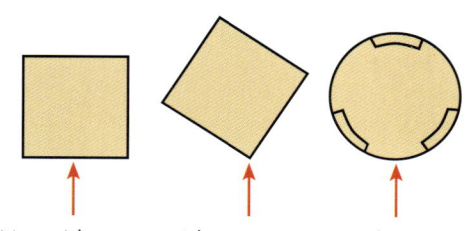

Use either one side or a corner of a square container as the front. In the case of a round container, two legs should face the viewer.

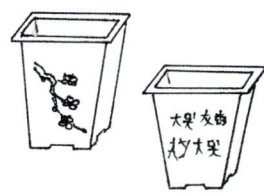

Cascade containers often have a floral design on the one side and an inscription, usually a haiku, on the other. For flowering or berry trees, the floral design faces the front. For evergreen trees, the inscription faces the front.

Display stands

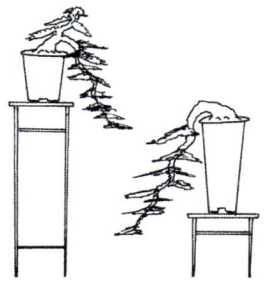

As a rule, tall stands are used for displaying cascades. However, if the container is very deep, a lower stand shows off the composition better.

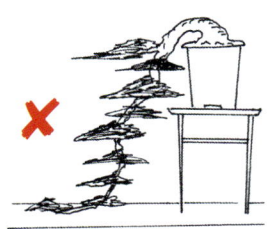

The tail end of the cascade must never touch the floor surface.

Plant material

Creepers such as bougainvillea, as well as hardwood groundcovers, i.e. the various low-spreading conifers and cotoneaster species are excellent cascade material. Most plant species can be used for the creation of semi-cascades. If deciduous plants are used for the creation of a full cascade, it often happens that the lower portion of the cascading branch dies back due to a lack of active sap flow.

The first leaves of this red-leaved fig (*Ficus ingens*) are almost coppery red and create a beautiful scene in spring. Height 30 cm.

Variations on basic styles

Broom style – Hoki-zukuri

Candle-flame style – Rosoku-zukuri

Pine-tree style – Matsu-zukuri

Willow or weeping style – Shidare-zukuri

Split trunk style – Sogu-ki

Gnarled trunk style – Bankan

Struck-by-lightning style – Kaminari

Strangler style

Hollow trunk style – Saba-miki

Elongated branch style – Tatami-mat

Coiled or twisted trunk style – Nejikan

A young *Celtis cinensis* grown in the broom style by die author. Height 40 cm.

Broom style – Hoki-zukuri

The broom style is one of the most delicate, and also one of the most beautiful styles found in bonsai art. Although this style appears formal, it radiates a feeling of tranquillity. The broom style reminds me of a dainty young lady, dressed in a wedding gown made of lace. It exudes an aura of softness not found in any of the other styles.

Deciduous trees are more suitable for this style, because one can admires their delicate branches and twiglets during winter when the trees have lost their leaves.

In an article on *Zelkova*, which appeared in *International Bonsai*, Autumn 1980, Lynn Perry Alstadt summed up her impression of the broom style as follows:

> *After nearly twenty years of living with my Zelkova, I am not sure if I take care of it by performing the daily ministering of its needs or if it takes care of me by providing that special peace of mind which comes from having looked at a work of art and found it satisfying, rewarding … inspiring.*

A *Zelkova serrata* covered with its cloak of autumn leaves. The *Zelkova serrata* is regarded as the finest example of the broom style. The rectangular container gives it a very formal appearance. Height 70 cm. Owner Mr Fusazo Takeyama of Omiya Japan.

The same tree in its winter bareness. Note the delicate branches and twiglets.

Guidelines for creating the classic broom style

Roots

 The surface roots are spread round the base to lead the eye upwards towards the delicate branch structure. Do not place the roots on one side of the trunk only as this placement will distract the viewer's attention from the beauty of the style.

Trunk line

The classic broom style always requires a formal trunk line and the trunk is smooth without any scars noticeable.

Interrupted trunk line

In the interrupted trunk line the trunk divides into a number of primary branches at roughly the same height above the ground. A soft, feminine appearance is the keystone of this style.

Continuous trunk line

The trunk line is uninterrupted from the base to the apex, which gives an impression of strength and masculinity.

Trunk length and size

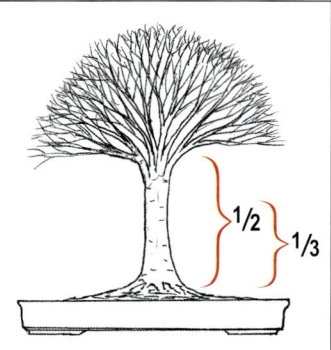

The trunk must not be too thick as a massive trunk does not look elegant. The length of the trunk may vary from one-third to about one-half the height of the tree.

Branch design

Symmetrical branch design

In the symmetrical design, the trunk divides into a number of primary branches at approximately the same height above the ground. The branch placement on the one side of the tree is a mirror image of the other side.

Asymmetrical branch design

In the asymmetrical design, the primary branches develop at different levels, and they sometimes vary in length.

Branch structure

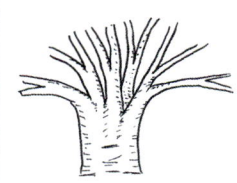

Two, three, five or seven primary branches normally form the branch structure of the interrupted trunk line design. The area from which the branches grow is smooth and even, but the thickness of the branches may vary.

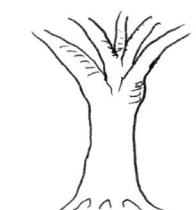

Branches taper towards the finest twig. Constant pruning results in twiggy growth. The branches of the broom style are long and straight, while those of the Pierneef style (see page 190) are zigzagged. Make sure that the branches always form a V-shape, as a U-shape destroys the beauty of the style.

Uncontrolled growth ruins the style and leads to an unattractive swollen base. Furthermore, the primary branches will grow out of proportion and destroy the delicacy of the style.

Silhouette lines

The silhouette line is of great importance to the total impact a style has on the viewer. The two main trunk lines, i.e. the interrupted and continuous trunk lines, have a direct influence on their separate silhouette lines.

The interrupted trunk line design

The upper silhouette of the interrupted trunk line design is either flat or round, while the lower silhouette line is either symmetrical or asymmetrical.

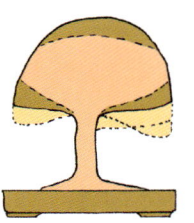

The continuous trunk line design

The upper silhouette line general varies from triangular to round, but the silhouette of the continuous trunk line design tends to be more triangular than that of the interrupted one.

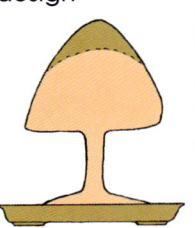

Variations on the classic broom style

Double trunk (Sokan)

Double trunks are quite common in nature. This is often prompted by an injury to the tip of a young seedling. The trunks are positioned slightly diagonally to avoid an open V-shape. For the best results, use only the continuous trunk line design.

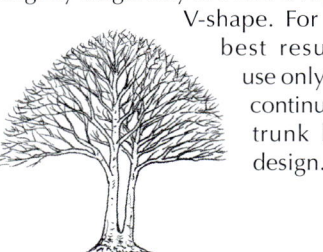

Twin trunk (Soju)

Most deciduous trees produce lots of seeds, with the result that twin trunks, or a number of trunks, are often produced. Trees with a continuous trunk line are planted in a diagonal position to create depth. The main tree is planted in front or at the back of the container. As the foliage of deciduous trees is less dense than that of evergreens, the branches can intermingle, and they are therefore not so susceptible to dying back.

Note: Although the broom style is delicate, it is still formal and cannot be trained into the slanting, cascading, root-over-rock or literati styles.

Variations on the informal broom style

Single trunk line

The informal broom style differs from the formal in that the branches are more curved and therefore less formal. The tree trunk is upright and carries the curved primary branches which culminate in a round crown. The trunk line usually has an interrupted design.

Short interrupted trunk line

The short tree trunk and three or five primary branches form the basic framework of this style. A shallow oval container adds to the beauty and delicateness of the composition.

Double trunk with a low-forked frame structure

Although the style is informal, the tree still appears soft and delicate.

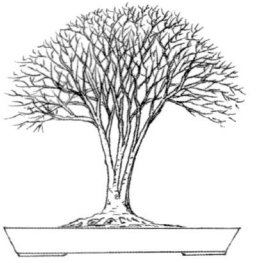

Interrupted trunk line with drooping branches

The branches droop slightly downwards to give a weeping effect. The round crown, however, gives the tree its broom shape.

Sprout broom style with drooping branches

The various main tree trunks split at the trunk base to form the sprout broom style. The fine growth droops softly downwards.

Containers

Oval or round containers are the most suitable for this style as they accentuate the movement of the round crowns. The depth of the container is usually equal to the girth of the trunk. The container is very shallow, as most trunks are thin and delicate. The length of the container is approximately equal to the circumference of the crown.

When using oval containers, plant the tree just off-centre and when using round containers plant the tree in the centre. To complement the tree in its winter bareness, use light-coloured containers.

Plant material

Deciduous trees are by far the most suitable for this style, such as elms, maples, *Celtis* (e.g. white stinkwoods or hackberries) and *Zelkova* which, according to the Japanese growers, is the prince of all broom styles. All these trees have the tendency to develop smooth, long branches which first fork into finer branches and eventually culminate in twiggy growth: this is the secret of the broom style. Small-leaved evergreen plant material can also be used but is not as fascinating as deciduous trees.

Candle-flame style – Rosoku-zukuri

The candle-flame style has a natural and delicate appearance. It is also called the 'little sister' of the broom style, but there are two main differences:

- Firstly, the candle-flame style and the broom style have different silhouette lines.
- Secondly, in the candle-flame style the branches are placed in an upright position, closer to the trunk than in the broom style.

The beauty of this Japanese beech is contained in the posture, with its grey-white unscarred trunk. One of the late Mr Iwasaki's precious trees.

Guidelines for creating the candle-flame style

Branch placement

Symmetrical branch placement

The continuous trunk line in this sketch has a shaped apex, symmetrical branch placement and the branches taper to form a lance.

Asymmetrical branch placement

The branches grow almost vertically upwards in the asymmetrical branch placement. This style is common among alder, beech, poplar, sweet gums (liquidambars) and ginkgo.

Variations on the candle-flame style

An old tree with a short trunk line

The continuous trunk line gives an impression of strength and stability.

Double trunk candle-flame style (Sokan)

Place the younger tree either in front of the older tree, or behind it. Never plant the two trunks next to each other because it will form an open 'V' which is unattractive. Always place the lowest branch on the smaller tree.

Twin-tree candle-flame style (Soju)

The twin-tree style is often referred to as 'Mr and Mrs Tree', because of the close relationship that exists between the two trees. Oval containers usually complement this style.

Triple-tree candle-flame style

The main trunk is placed in the centre and the two minor trunks in a supporting position. The oval container contributes towards the tranquillity of the scene.

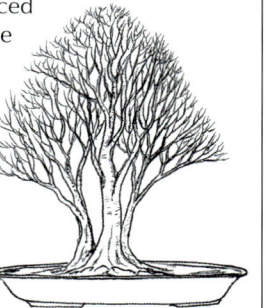

Typical growing pattern of the ginkgo

The branches grow almost vertically upwards against the trunk, thereby concealing the main trunk. A deep oval container has been chosen to balance the thick tree trunk.

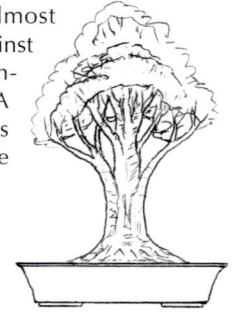

Silhouette line

The silhouette line resembles a burning flame. The lower silhouette line can be symmetrical or asymmetrical.

Containers

To complement the columnar shape of the style, use dish-like or oval containers.

Plant material

To accentuate the delicate appearance of the style, use deciduous plants with small leaves, e.g. elms, maples, ginkgo, beech, ash, alder, oaks and *Celtis* species. Evergreens with small leaves and conifers may also be used. It stands to reason that plants with broad leaves and trees with compound leaves are not suitable.

Pine-tree style – Matsu-zukuri

According to John Naka, the pine tree is one of the most popular shapes, and one into which almost any tree can be styled. To quote John: 'Because of this majestic shape, it has become a representative of something philosophical as well as something beautiful.' The pine-tree shape is similar to the informal upright style, except that it has a specific structure. The triangular form is dominant, which is a typical oriental feature.

This Japanese five-needle pine is an excellent example of the pine-tree style. The tree belonged to the late Mr Iwasaki.

Guidelines for creating the pine-tree style

Basic structure

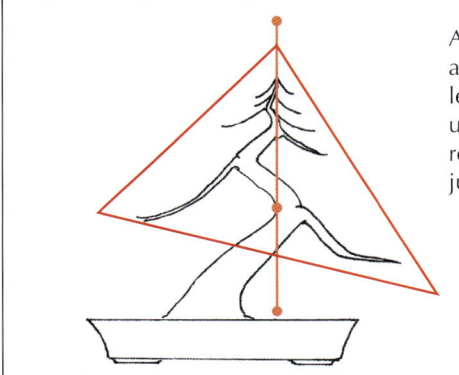

An inclined lower trunk, which zigzags towards the apex and a traditional branch arrangement, i.e. a right, back, left and front, form the basic framework. Branches are usually formed on the outside of the curves in the trunk; roots are well spread round the trunk, and the apex is just off-centre from the trunk base.

Elegant pine shape

The trunk curves softly towards the apex, and the primary branches are placed on the outside of the curves in the trunk. The tree emanates a feeling of strength and stability. The movement of the trunk line is reflected in the soft lines of the oval container.

Traditional pine-tree style

Most conifers can be shaped into the pine-tree style because of their formal appearance. They also radiate a masculine mood, and the leaves can be kept well within the limits of the triangle. To set off the trunk, and to add to the feeling of stability, a deep rectangular container has been selected.

Jins and shari's

By using jins and shari's a struggle for survival can be captured, as is shown in this sketch. The straight lines of the container contrast well with the movement of the tree.

Deciduous trees

The pine shape is ideal for deciduous trees such as maples, elms and *Celtis* species. Compactness and tidiness are two distinct features of this style, although the total impact is one of naturalness. A deep oval container not only matches the trunk's circumference, but also emphasises its flow.

Plant material

Although any plant material may be used, conifers are the most suitable for this style.

Willow or weeping style – Shidare-zukuri

The Japanese regard the willow as the strongest tree, because not even strong winds can break its branches. Although gentle and soft in appearance, it sometimes withstands gale-force winds by giving way to the wind, only to return to its original position after the storm has subsided.

As the willow is usually associated with country streams, rivers and marshland, its beauty and grace evoke a feeling of softness and tranquillity.

The weeping style is determined by the drooping manner of the branches and not by the inclination of the tree trunk, as is the case in the other styles.

All basic styles can be reshaped into the weeping style except for the formal upright (Chokkan), because the informal branch structure of the willow looks artificial on a formal upright trunk. As one associates the tree with water, it should not be planted over a rock.

A tamarisk tree trained in the willow or weeping style by Mr Thanun Thanun.

Guidelines for creating the weeping style

Trunk

The trunk has to be strong and stable so that it can carry the long secondary branches cascading down from the primary branches.

Primary branches

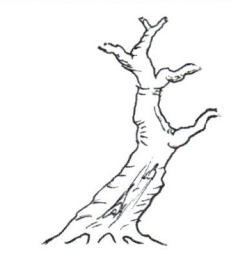

The lower portion of the primary branch must grow upwards, because the primary branch has to carry the secondary and the tertiary weeping branches.

Secondary branches

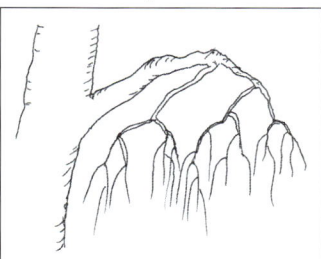

Prune secondary branches; train them into semi-circles with the help of wire, and make sure that the tips point almost vertically downwards. Also train all lower branches into semi-circles.

Possible Shidare-zukuri styles

Informal Shidare

This old tree has an arched form. To complement this shape, use a round container, as shown in the sketch.

Slanting Shidare

This peaceful design evokes a feeling of tranquillity. The shallow oval container rounds off the scene.

Slanting and semi-cascade Shidare

The overhanging branch brings to mind a rustic scene, where a tree is growing at the edge of a pool. This is a popular style for the weeping cherry. A deep round container must be used to accommodate the weeping branch.

Full cascade Shidare

The full cascade Shidare is extremely suitable for flowering plants such as *Wisteria* and winter jasmine. The cascading branch is best displayed in a deep cascade container.

Weeping style with a hollow trunk – Saba-miki

The weeping style with a hollow trunk is a combination often seen in nature, and one worth trying. A deep oval container complements this composition.

Plant material

Plants suitable for this style are: willow, *Tamarix*, *Ficus benjamini*, weeping cherry, some teabush species (*Leptospermum*), *Buddleja saligna* and *Myrtus communis*, as well as some herb species such as lavender and thyme.

A pepper tree (*Schinus molle*) trained in the willow style by Erika Köhler.

88

Split trunk style – Sogu-ki

The split trunk style is often found in nature, for instance, lightning often splits a single trunk into two, or strong winds sometimes tear heavy trunks apart. Always keep in mind that the end result must look natural, even though the tree is split artificially.

A wild olive (*Olea europaea* subsp. *africana*) displaying the mood of the split tree trunk style. The tree belongs to Mr Gus Umberto.

Guidelines for creating the split trunk style

Split by lightning

This formal upright design depicts a tree that has been split in two by lightning. Always place the first branch on the shorter trunk and jinn the apex of this trunk for a natural split-by-lightning appearance.

The giant baobab in this dramatic double-trunk style depicts a tree struck by lightning. A deep rectangular container, which gives stability to the creation, has been used.

Split by strong winds

Informal split trunk

This sketch shows an informally styled tree trunk split by strong winds. The split in the trunk must be well defined to give an illusion of a tree torn in half by a mighty storm.

Slanting split trunk style

This creation gives an impression of a trunk that was split and blown down by strong winds. The two trunks form a harmonious composition. But remember: (a) the major trunk is always thicker than the minor trunk, and (b) the foliage mass of the major trunk is always greater than that of the minor trunk.

Split root base

The root base has been split to simulate a well-known redwood tree in the Yosemite National Park, called Needle Pin. To complement the composition, a long rectangular container is used.

Containers

Oval or rectangular containers may be used for this style. The container should always be in proportion to the circumference of the trunk.

Plant material

You may use any suitable plant material.

A split trunk tree in nature, this impressive redwood pine tree can be found in the Yosemite National Park, California.

90

Gnarled trunk style – Bankan

The gnarled trunk style is seldom seen in bonsai collections, because suitable plant material is very difficult to find. For instance, a plant with a thick trunk as well as a gnarled and battered appearance is seldom found in nature.

Even though a tree can be transformed into one of the basic styles, the rugged appearance of the gnarled and disfigured trunk is so dominant that the basic style is of little importance.

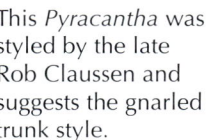

This *Pyracantha* was styled by the late Rob Claussen and suggests the gnarled trunk style.

Guidelines for creating the gnarled trunk style

The trunk must appear old, and signs of aging must be visible on its bark, knobs and crevices. Although the tree has a rugged appearance, and seems to dominate the scene, the overall impression must still be one of softness and gentleness. A deep rectangular container is recommended, as it emphasises the rugged and gnarled effect.

This deciduous tree gives the impression of suffering and hardship in its struggle for survival – droughts and windstorms could have damaged the branches, or perhaps elephants, in an attempt to reach for fruit or leaves, could have broken the branches.

The gnarled trunk looks best in a deep oval container.

Struck-by-lightning style – Kaminari

In nature one often finds that trees growing on high mountains are struck by lightning. The force of the bolt of lightning is sometimes so severe that the tree is either split in half or a part thereof is damaged.

The section from the apex down to where the bark is burnt and peeled off, is called *shari*. This style can be very interesting and dramatic. One must take care, however, not to create an artificial effect.

This *Pemphis acidula* was created by Robert Steven and is an excellent example of the struck-by-lightning style. Height 65 cm.

Guidelines for creating the struck-by-lightning style

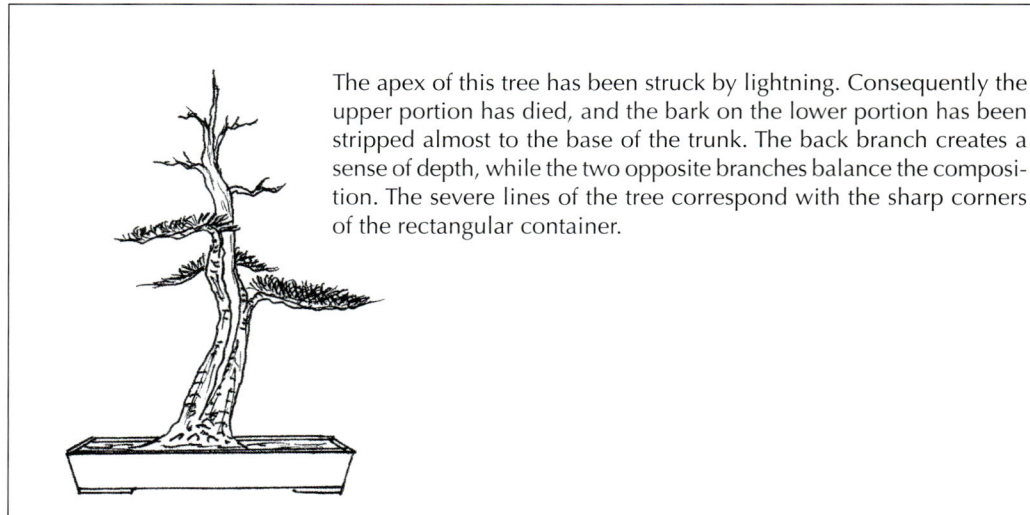

The apex of this tree has been struck by lightning. Consequently the upper portion has died, and the bark on the lower portion has been stripped almost to the base of the trunk. The back branch creates a sense of depth, while the two opposite branches balance the composition. The severe lines of the tree correspond with the sharp corners of the rectangular container.

Only the primary branch is left after lightning has struck the tree, and this branch is then trained into a semi-cascade literati style. A round literati container complements the composition.

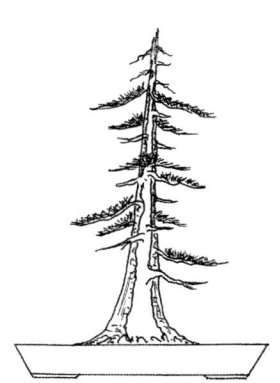

Lightning has burnt a path through the centre of this tree, and most of its branches have died. The emphasis is placed on the jins and shari's. To avoid a monotonous effect, you can alternate jins with live branches, and jin the apexes to create a natural effect, as lightning always strikes from top to bottom.

Containers

The struck-by-lightning style is dramatic, therefore select containers which will emphasise movement or the mood of the tree. Oval, round or rectangular containers are the most suitable.

Plant material

Deciduous trees do not grow at high altitudes, therefore select only evergreens such as pines and conifers for the style (avoid broad-leaved varieties). As the total impact of the style is one of suffering, make sure that the foliage is sparse.

Strangler style

In tropical areas we find that many *Ficus* species are stranglers, as they have the habit and ability to use other trees as their hosts. Unfortunately, the host eventually dies due to the impact the roots of the strangler tree have on the lifeline of the host tree.

The strangler phenomenon occurs all over the world where strangler figs grow, but it is not limited to the *Ficus* species – the rata (*Metrosideros robusta*) from New Zealand is an excellent example of a completely different species that does exactly the same.

A swamp fig (*Ficus trichopoda*) wrapped around its host tree, slowly strangling it.

The seeds of strangler plants are deposited mainly through faeces of animals – usually monkeys and birds – into crevices and openings in the bark of the host tree where they germinate. The strangler plant has the unique ability, vigour and power to continue growth, sending aerial roots down the trunk of the host tree to finally anchor itself in the soil around its base.

The invader is an epiphyte and not a parasite as it does not use any nutrients from the host. It uses the host as an anchor and support, only to eventually suffocate it to death with its powerful roots, devouring it like a python does its prey. When the host tree dies, it leaves an enormous upright strangler with a hollow core.

The strangling process can be broken down into three distinct and clearly identifiable phases: the invader phase, the strangling phase and the victor phase. To stand in the presence of one of these trees in nature, imagining the entire process – from the opportunistic invasion of the host, to slowly and cunningly strangling it and finally emerging as the triumphant victor – is simply fascinating.

This *Ficus burtt davyi* by Dr Tobie Kleynhans is an excellent example of the strangler style.

Guidelines for creating the strangler style

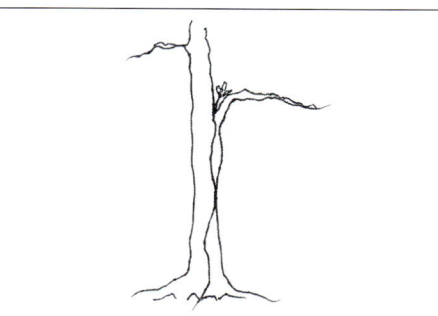

During phase 1, the seed sends down its aerial root to anchor the plant in the soil.

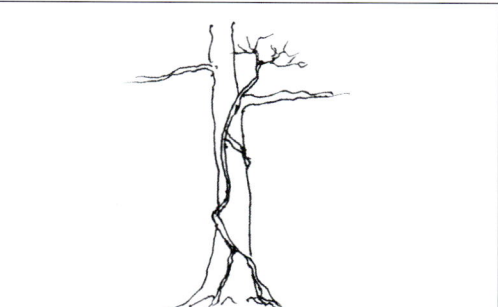

During phase 2, the young strangler seed starts to grow on the host tree, using it as a support.

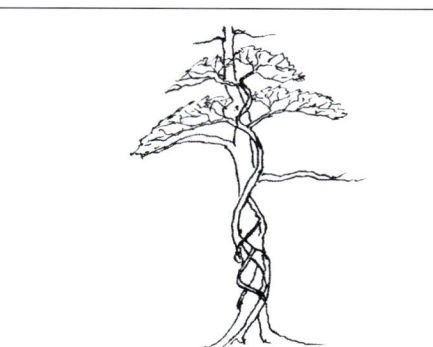

This process continues as the roots of the strangler start to coil around the host tree.

During the final phase the strangler completely takes over the host tree, finally strangling it to death.

Containers

Oval or round containers, slightly deeper than normal, will balance the thick trunk formed by the aerial roots.

Plant material

Most of the *Ficus* species that form aerial roots are suitable for this style.

The strangler style was inspired by Mac Boshoff, one of South Africa's leading bonsai growers. This is one of his creations.

Hollow trunk style – Saba-miki

Fungi, termites, trunk borers or animals such as elephants in search of water, may be the cause of a hollow trunk. Sometimes the giant baobabs are hollowed out by local people who use the hollow areas for homes or storing space.

Most of the basic styles can be used for the hollow trunk style, but delicate trees or styles, such as the broom or literati, are unsuitable. Trees with thick trunks lend themselves well to the creation of the style.

Avoid hollowing the tree up to soil level as the trunk can rot and damage your tree.

The focal point of this outstanding hollow trunk style has been captured the rectangular container. This holm oak belonged to the late Mr Iwasaki.

Guidelines for creating the hollow trunk style

Formal upright Saba-miki

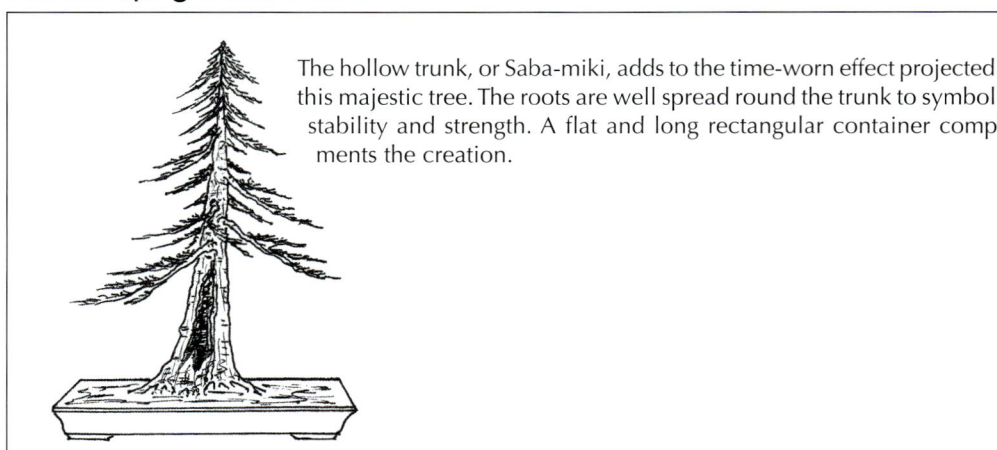

The hollow trunk, or Saba-miki, adds to the time-worn effect projected by this majestic tree. The roots are well spread round the trunk to symbolise stability and strength. A flat and long rectangular container complements the creation.

Informal Saba-miki

Hollow trunks are sometimes caused by termites. In bonsai the hollow area should preferably not extend down to the root base, to prevent the trunk from rotting. The hollow trunk is usually found only on the first third portion of the trunk. A classic incurved rectangular container complements this creation.

Willow Saba-miki

A hollow trunk often occurs in a willow tree, because its wood is very soft and susceptible to rotting. Despite the hollow trunk, the tree still radiates a feeling of strength. The oval container conforms to the movement of the hollow trunk.

Baobab Saba-miki

The hollow in the trunk adds to the dramatic impact which this giant tree has on the viewer. The deep oval container accentuates the movement of the tree.

Containers

Oval or rectangular containers may be used in accordance with the plant's overall silhouette and trunk width.

Plant material

Any of the small-leafed trees with thick trunks may be used for this style. Hardwood species are more suitable, because softwood species tend to rot very easily. However, lime sulphur or ordinary wood glue can be used to preserve the wood.

A bougainvillea created in the hollow trunk style by Mac MacDonald of Durban.

97

Elongated branch style – Tatami-mat

This unique style is often called the coat-hanger or Tatami-mat style. The Japanese simply regard it as a variation of the informal upright style.

As the name indicates, the first branch is over-developed and breaks away from the trunk, similar to a sucker that wants to take over. This occurs in nature when most of the energy is pumped into the first branch while the rest of the tree develops later to its full capacity. The elongated branch style resembles the double-trunk style, with the exception that the first branch grows out horizontally and not vertically.

The style is often found amongst trees growing on the edge of a cliff or over a rocky dome. The heat of the rock also contributes to the over-development of the low branch. Although the style is not often seen in bonsai collections, it is beautiful and therefore worth trying.

An outstanding example of the elongated branch style by Mr Mikio Oshima; it was later given as a birthday present to Chase Rosade.

Guidelines for creating the elongated branch style

Low-spreading primary branch in an upward position

The design depicts a tree growing on top of a mountain, and which is being buffeted by uprising winds. The main roots are well spread out and one of the major roots is placed under the primary branch to emphasise the tension in the branch movement.

Low-spreading primary branch in a downward position

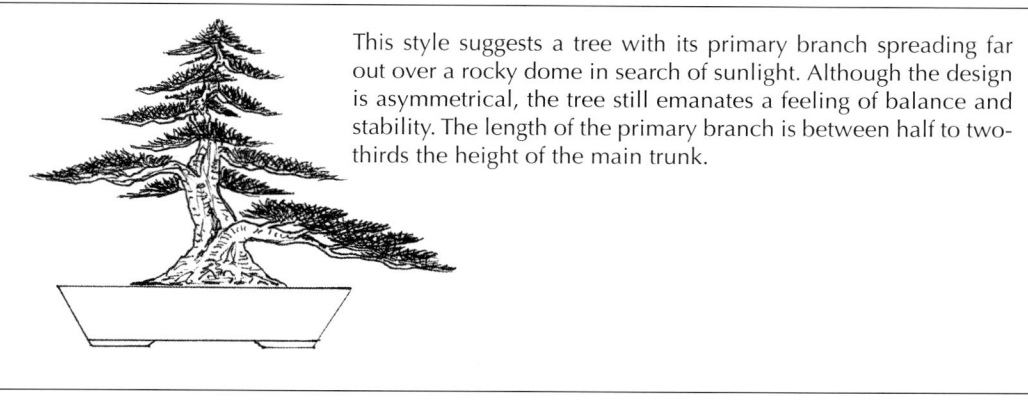

This style suggests a tree with its primary branch spreading far out over a rocky dome in search of sunlight. Although the design is asymmetrical, the tree still emanates a feeling of balance and stability. The length of the primary branch is between half to two-thirds the height of the main trunk.

Deciduous trees

Deciduous trees such as oaks and elms – but also evergreens such as conifers, pines, olives, wild figs and *Buddlejas* – can be shaped into the elongated branch style with great success.

This tree radiates a masculine power that is pleasing to the eye.

This is another informal deciduous tree with a long-stretching primary branch. To create this low-growing style, the main trunk must be kept short, and the crown compact, hence an impression of strength and stability will be achieved. A deep rectangular container adds to the effect of stability.

Slanting elongated branch style

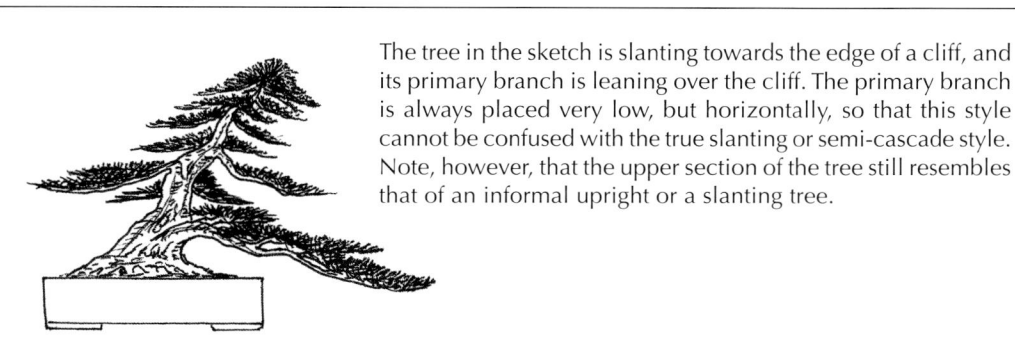

The tree in the sketch is slanting towards the edge of a cliff, and its primary branch is leaning over the cliff. The primary branch is always placed very low, but horizontally, so that this style cannot be confused with the true slanting or semi-cascade style. Note, however, that the upper section of the tree still resembles that of an informal upright or a slanting tree.

Broad-crowned tree

Another slanting position, but the crown is broader and rounder than the one in the previous sketch. The tip never droops lower than the edge of the container, otherwise it becomes a semi-cascade style.

Some well-known examples of this style

The following sketches depict the most famous elongated branch styles created by the late Mr Saichi Suzuki.

The most famous of all elongated branch styles is probably this Japanese five-needle pine (*Pinus parviflora zuisho*), with the impressive name of Ryu-ho, meaning dragon or phoenix. The tree belonged to the late Mr Saichi Suzuki who was also known as the father of *Zuisho*, a subspecies of the Japanese black pine. Mr Suzuki was regarded by bonsai masters as the foremost authority on conifers, especially the Japanese black and five-needle pines.

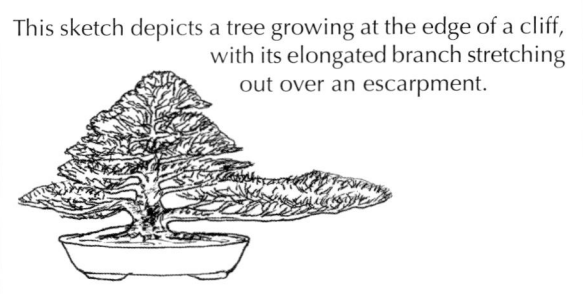

This sketch depicts a tree growing at the edge of a cliff, with its elongated branch stretching out over an escarpment.

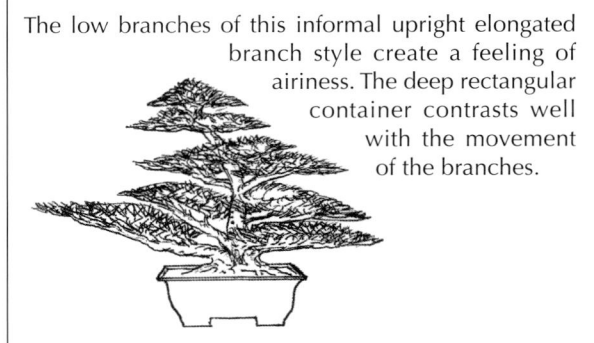

The low branches of this informal upright elongated branch style create a feeling of airiness. The deep rectangular container contrasts well with the movement of the branches.

Containers

More emphasis is placed on the elongated branch when the tree is planted in a deep square, hexagonal or round container. Furthermore, by placing the focus on the asymmetrical balance of the creation, another artistic dimension is added.

Plant material

Conifers, olives, *Buddleja*, *Schotia* and *Ficus* species, as well as small-leafed deciduous plant material with a thick trunk base and a dominant low-forking primary branch, are suitable for this style.

Coiled or twisted trunk style – Nejikan

This is an unusual style that is seldom seen in bonsai collections. The origin of the style can be as a result of plant material exposed to strong seasonal winds blowing clockwise from one direction to the other throughout the various seasons. The California juniper is a good example of this phenomenon.

Another explanation for the origin of the style is vines coiling round an object in search for sunlight. The trunk base of old vines such as *Wisteria* and jasmine can therefore effectively be utilised for this interesting style.

This Shimpaku juniper is an outstanding example of the coiled trunk style. It was styled by Mr Katsumi Yasuri and owned by the late Mr Iwasaki.

Guidelines for creating the coiled trunk style

Root base

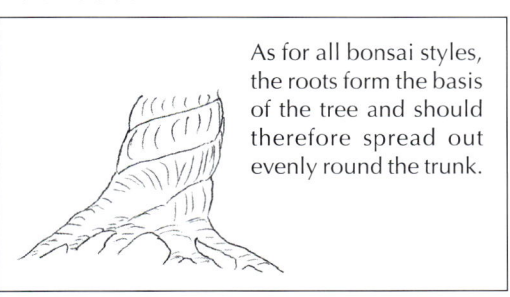

As for all bonsai styles, the roots form the basis of the tree and should therefore spread out evenly round the trunk.

Trunk

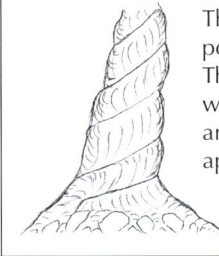

The trunk forms the focal point of this particular style. The coils should curve upwards in an informal way and must taper towards the apex.

101

Variations on the coiled style

Informal coiled style

As the total impact of the style is informal, the tree should also be trained informally. The basic rules for the informal style also apply to the coiled style. Although the curves of the trunk and branches blend in well with the movement of an oval container, an interesting contrast is created with the straight lines of the rectangular container.

Slanting coiled style

The tree is planted to the side of the container to create depth and movement. An oval container complements the movement of the coiled style.

Double-trunk coiled style

Strong winds were possibly responsible for this dramatic creation of a double trunk. To blend in with the broad base, a deep rectangular container has been selected to contrast with the movement of the trunk.

Literati coiled style

The dainty coils of this literati styled tree evoke a feeling of movement and spaciousness, almost like a ballerina going through her paces. A hexagonal container rounds off the composition.

Artificially coiled style

The coiled or spiral style can also be formed artificially by stripping the bark of a tree in a spiral around the trunk. Great care should, however, be taken to follow the live vein of the tree. As the creation suggests a tree battling for survival, the foliage should be sparse and not too lustrous.

Containers

Although oval containers are normally suited to this style, the sharp and straight lines of rectangular containers often form an interesting contrast with the movement of the trunk.

Plant material

If old vine understock is available, it is the ideal material to start the style off. Conifers such as the California juniper occur naturally in the Nevada Desert and are a wonderful source of plant material for bonsai growers in that particular region of the world.

Rock settings

Root-over-rock style – Seki-jo-ju
Clinging-to-the-rock style – Ishi-zuke

This trident maple was styled by Mr Kiku Shinkai and was later acquired by the late Mr Iwasaki. The photos show the tree in its summer and autumn colours.

Mountain peaks, deep ravines, vertical cliffs and rugged rock formations usually have an overwhelming effect on most viewers. The impressiveness of rock formations is only to be admired by nature's noblest creation – mankind. No wonder that the Chinese and, even more so, the Japanese regard rocks as the highest form of nature's creation. Rocks can very effectively be used in bonsai styling, as the next two styles will show.

Root-over-rock style – Seki-jo-ju

In the root-over-rock style the tree is planted on the rock, with its roots straggling downwards until they reach the soil.

Most of the well-known styles can be transformed into this style. Various approaches such as the near view (close-up) or the distant view can be created. It is not difficult to master this style – the only difficulty is to find interesting and characterful rocks.

The roots form the focal point of this old sycamore fig planted over a rock in 1972 by the author. Through constant pruning, the leaves reduced by two-thirds their normal size. This tree was selected as one of the 100 best trees in the world by the Nippon Bonsai Society in 2001. Height 48 cm.

Guidelines for creating the root-over-rock style

Selection of rock

The base of the rock must:
- be stable
- have six planes: front, back, top and bottom, as well as a left and a right side.

The surface of the rock must:
- be rough
- have enough crevices in which the roots can grow downwards.

The rock must have:
- character
- many nesting places into which the trees can settle
- an average size of approximately 20 cm in circumference at the base and 25 cm in height.

Hints for selecting a rock

- The rock should not be round, square or symmetrical, as this will look unnatural.
- Do not select a rock that is too heavy, as it will make handling difficult.
- Dark rocks are preferred over light-coloured rocks.
- Avoid rocks formed of compressed sand, such as sandstone, as they will not be durable.
- Discard any rocks that have fresh breaks.

Roots

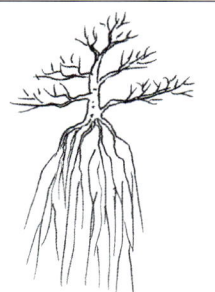

The tap-root is removed well in advance to encourage the formation of a homologous and well-spread root system. If the tap-root is not removed, it will overpower the rest of the roots and the side roots will not develop fully.

For a natural appearance, the roots must cling tightly to the rock, as open spaces between roots and rock not only look unnatural, but also distract the viewer's attention from the beauty of the creation.

Do not use trees with strong main roots as the roots will be too hard to bend. Furthermore, they will not make contact with the rock and the end result will be unattractive. To avoid this problem always select young trees with flexible roots. Natural rock-clinging trees, like the wild fig species, are by far the best choice.

Trunk

As the rock now takes over the role of the trunk, the trunk is kept short and the branches are placed low to serve as side branches for the rock base.

A formal upright tree should never be planted on an informal rock structure. The trunk should always be informal to harmonise with the informal rock base.

A long narrow rock acts as a trunk for this root-over-rock style. The style of the tree can be either informal upright or slanting, depending on the shape of the rock. To achieve a natural effect, the tree has to follow the movement of the rock.

Near-view approach

In the near-view approach the tree is in a dominant position while the rock is in a subordinate position.

Informal root-over-rock style

The tree is planted half-way up the rock, with its trunk leaning over the rock. The lower branches are cascading down the rock as if they were protecting it. A deep oval container of average size completes the scene.

Slanting root-over-rock style

The tree is planted on the rock, with its roots covering most of the rock. The primary branch cascades downwards to give balance to the composition. It is imperative to have back branches to give depth to the composition.

Extreme slanting root-over-rock style

This tree follows the movement of the rock. The first branch cascades over the cliff, but the balancing branch grows away from the slant. To capture the movement of the composition, a shallow oval container has been selected.

Pine shape root-over-rock style

The apex of the tree is positioned just off the centre of the trunk base. The broad base of the rock helps to create an impression of elegance and maturity. Choose an oval or a round container to emphasise the trunk's movement.

Triple-trunk root-over-rock planting

This scene suggests trees growing on a rocky dome. Although the outside trunks are facing in opposite directions, the upper lines follow the same movement. A long oval container adds to the feeling of spaciousness.

Yose-uye root-over-rock style

The sketch shows an informal group of trees planted on top of a rock, with the trees leaning sideways in search of as much sunlight as possible. Remember that a formal group of trees should never be planted on a rock, because a rock is always treated as an informal base. The straight lines of the container contrast well with the informal lines of the rock and trunks.

Windswept root-over-rock style

In this near-view composition the tree dominates the rock. A feeling of desolation has been captured by emphasising the jins, hence only a few living branches are allowed. For good effect, keep the foliage sparse.

Rock-and-tree composition

In this composition the rock acts as a partner, hence the tree follows the same movement as the rock. The tree is planted on the lower rock base from which the roots cascade into the soil. The branch placement is the same as that of a single tree, i.e., there are branches in front and at the back of the rock to give an illusion of depth.

Distant-view approach

In the distant-view approach the emphasis is on the rock and not on the tree.

To enable the branches of the tree to cascade down, place the tree either in the centre or two-thirds up the rock.

Windswept root-over-rock style

To create a windswept effect, plant the tree halfway down the rock, and keep the foliage sparse, to emphasise the struggle against the elements. Conifers are ideal plant material.

Slanting root-over-rock style

To accentuate the crest of the rocky mountain, the tree is slanting away from the crest. Conifers and small-leafed trees may be used. It is essential, however, to keep the trees in proportion to the size of the rock. In contrast to the Ishi-zuki style, the roots in this style are cascading down the rock into the soil.

Containers

Use shallow oval, round or rectangular containers, and make sure that the colour of the container blends in with the colour of the rock. Your best choice will be earthen-coloured containers.

Plant material

Ficus species are by far the best choice for the root-over-rock style as they are natural rock lovers. Other small-leafed plants like conifers, *Olea* and *Buddleja* species, as well as deciduous plants such as elm, maple and *Celtis* species are ideal for the Seki-jo-ju style.

Clinging-to-the-rock style – Ishi-zuke

Sometimes we see a cloud that's dragonish;
A vapour sometime like a bear or lion,
A tower'd citadel, a pendant rock,
A forked mountain, or blue promontory
With trees upon't.

Shakespeare: *Anthony and Cleopatra*

The clinging-to-the-rock, or Ishi-zuke, is one of the most impressive styles in bonsai. It can be compared with Saikai – the art of landscaping, a sister art of bonsai. In landscaping, for instance, a scene is created on a tray, whereas in this style the artist's aim is to simulate a mountain landscape, hence the rock, and not the tree, is the most important feature.

This is a good example of the clinging-to-the-rock style. Note that the trees must not overpower the rock. This creation belongs to Dr Koos le Roux.

Guidelines for creating the clinging-to-the-rock style

Selection of rock

The rock must have:

- character
- many crevices, to act as planting areas
- a craggy texture
- a three-dimensional appearance (i.e., a left and a right side, and an interesting front and back)
- a weathered appearance on all sides – one must be able to view the rock from all sides.

The shape, texture and colour of the rock must be kept in mind when selecting the best side for the front. The grooves in the rock must flow almost vertically upwards. Horizontal lines look unnatural, avoid them.

The rock base must be stable so that it can be displayed on its own or in a flat container. The base can be stabilised by using epoxy cement and gluing the base onto a stone with a similar texture. Note that the end result must always look natural.

Hints for selecting a rock

- The rock must be manageable – it must not be too big to carry.
- No fresh breaks or man-made cuts must be visible anywhere on the rock.
- Limestone and sandstone are not suitable – they will disintegrate with regular watering.
- Do not use round or smooth rocks.
- Hard rocks such as granite and dolomite, e.g. the Pelindaba rock, are most suitable.

Plant placement

Use the best features of the rock as a focal point. Place the trees in more or less the same positions as shown in the sketch, to accentuate the features of the rock. Do not plant any trees on top of the rock.

Ensure that the trees are small in relation to the rock. Vary the size of the plants from 5 cm to 10 cm if, for instance, the height of the rock is approximately 35 cm.

Here the focus is on the steep cliff, therefore the trees are placed on the longest side of the rock to form a triangle. This principle can be used very effectively in the Ishi-zuke style. Do not add too much detail to the trees as they are meant to be seen from a distance. Make sure, however, that all trunks and surface roots are visible.

Do not be tempted into using all the crevices as planting areas. Rather use the uninteresting crevices as planting areas, and leave the interesting ones for the viewer to admire. The container is usually filled with coarse river sand or water, depending on the scene the artist wants to simulate.

Distant-view approach

Distant mountain or Toyama

Keep the trees small in relation to the mountain, as the aim is to simulate a distant mountain landscape.

Island rock or Shima-gata

The flat rock simulates an island while the water and coarse sand in the container suggest the sea.

Sentinel rock or Dan-ishi

The rock extends into the air like a sentinel. The quartz strip in the centre of the rock suggests a waterfall, also called Taki-ishi. Trees are planted at varying heights to give special emphasis to the tall rock. Coarse sand is landscaped in front of the quartz strip to simulate a pool of water.

Shelter from rain or Ama-yadori-ishi

The rock simulates an overhanging cliff, with a tree cascading over its edge.

Rocky sea-shore

The two rocks suggest a rocky sea-shore and the white sand suggests waves crashing against the rocks. A feeling of barrenness and isolation is conveyed by this scene.

110

Near-view approach

In this near-view approach the focus is on the trees, but the rock remains a prominent feature. The trees are taller than those being used in the distant-view approach and greater attention is given to detail. As in all Ishi-zuke styles, the trees are planted in hollow crevices and the roots do not reach the base of the container.

In this near-view planting the rock forms the focal point, hence it should not be over-planted. The trees serve only as a background.

In this cascade Ishi-zuke growing down a cliff, there is complete harmony between rock and tree. The movement of the rock is captured in the cascading branches. A dish-like container gives an airy feeling to the creation.

Containers

Choose flat, oval or rectangular containers for this style. Do not put drainage holes in the pots as they will be filled with either water, to suggest an island or a sea landscape, or coarse river sand to round off the scene.

Plant material

The compact, fibrous root systems of hardy plants such as conifers, *Olea*, *Buddleja* and certain small-leafed *Ficus* species (especially *Ficus burtt davyii* 'Nana') are able to penetrate into the crevices in the rock, therefore they can withstand the dryer conditions better than plants with a poor root system. Moisture-loving plants like elms, maples and *Celtis* species cannot cope with dry conditions.

The miniature plant species available at nurseries are highly recommended. Some excellent species are *Cotoneaster microphylla*, *Euonymus microphyllus*, *Lonicera nitida*, *Serissa foetida*, *Myrtus communis* and *Buxus microphylla*. These species are also ideal for distant-view settings. A combination of plants may be used, but make sure that their requirements are the same. Indigenous plants, various conifers, succulents, or even interesting small grasses, make good combinations.

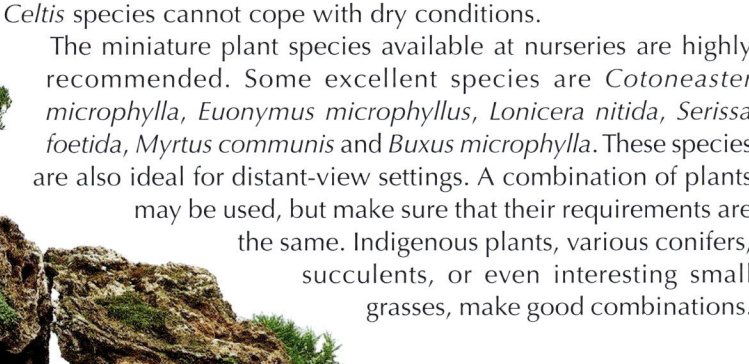

This is a fine example of a tree-on-the-rock style by Mr Thanun Thanun.

Styles originating from a single root system

Double-trunk style – Sokan

Fallen tree or raft style – Ikadabuki

Root-connected or sinuous style – Netsuranari

Turtle-back or stump style – Korabuki

Clump or sprout style – Kabudachi

This young flowering tea bush (*Leptospermum scoparium*) by Mr Colin Gerrans is a fine example of the double-trunk style.

Double-trunk style – Sokan

The Sokan style is one of the many beautiful styles in bonsai, and symbolises total harmony and companionship between two partners. This relationship could be between perhaps a happy married couple, a father and son, mother and daughter, etc.

The difference between the Sokan and Soju styles is that in the Sokan style the trees share the same root system, whereas in the Soju or twin-trunk style (see page 151), two separate trees are planted closely together.

Although two is a prime number and regarded by the Japanese as uneven, the dual-planting is the only exception to be used in the Sokan and Soju styles.

This outstanding double trunk (*Juniperus sabina chinensis*) forms part of the collection of the Yi Ran Gardens in China.

Guidelines for creating the double trunk style

Root system

The surface roots spread out evenly round the base. The strongest roots, however, sprout from the main trunk.

Trunk and base

The trunk divides at ground level, or very close to the base.

Trunk size

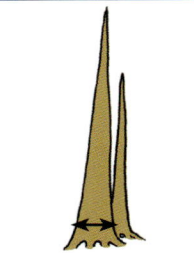

The major trunk is at least twice the size of the minor trunk.

Height of the tree

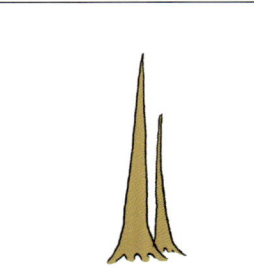

The major tree is at least one-third taller than the minor tree.

Visual weight

The visual weight of the major tree should be two-thirds the size of the minor tree.

Positioning of the trunks

It is not important which of the two trunks is in front. The important requirement is that it must create depth. The trunk's position should always be slightly diagonal.

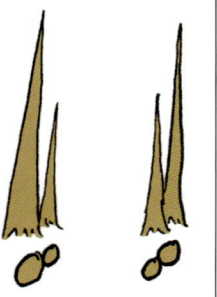

Harmony and trunk movement

The movement of the minor trunk is normally the same as that of the major tree.

Although these two trunks move in opposite directions, the apexes follow the same direction.

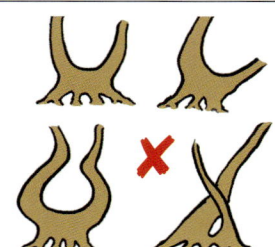

Avoid the following common faults:
- 'U'-shaped or half-moon trunk lines (top sketches)
- knock-kneed and crossed trunk lines (bottom sketches).

Branch arrangement

The branch placement for the Sokan style is arranged in the same way as for a single tree. Branches are arranged, as far as possible, according to the 'rule of three'. It can therefore be right, back and left. The next arrangement could then be front, right and back, etc.

The first and lowest branch is normally on the smallest tree, while the first branch on the major tree is on the opposite side of the minor tree.

The first third of the major tree's trunk is free of branches, except when the minor tree is growing in a semi-cascade.

There should be enough space between the apex of the minor tree and the branch directly above it. The top branch is also kept short to allow for enough sunlight.

The lowest branches should not be on the same level.

Possible double-trunk styles

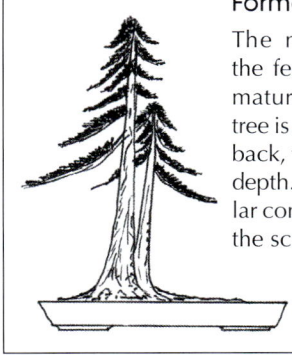

Formal Sokan

The major tree evokes the feeling of an old and matured tree. The minor tree is placed slightly to the back, to give the necessary depth. A shallow rectangular container complements the scene.

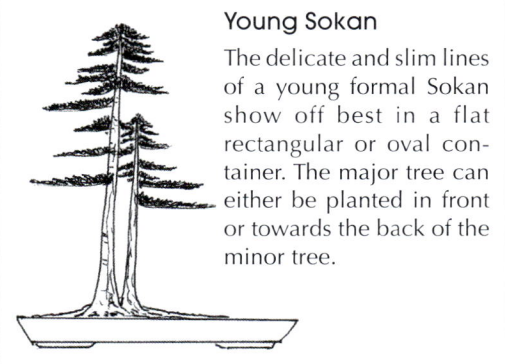

Young Sokan

The delicate and slim lines of a young formal Sokan show off best in a flat rectangular or oval container. The major tree can either be planted in front or towards the back of the minor tree.

Informal Sokan

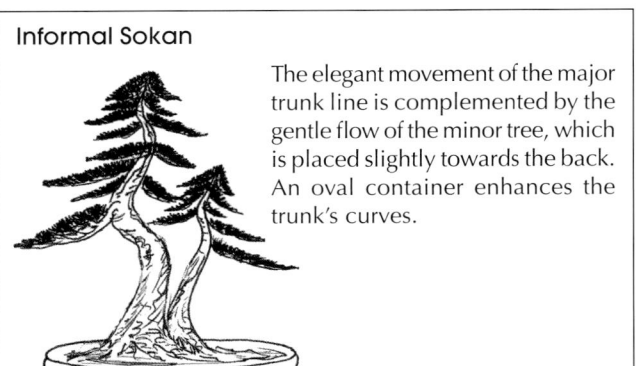

The elegant movement of the major trunk line is complemented by the gentle flow of the minor tree, which is placed slightly towards the back. An oval container enhances the trunk's curves.

Pine-shape Sokan

The trunk movement of the two trees complement each other. The minor tree is placed in the foreground as to support the older tree. The curvaceous legs of the container emphasise the movement of the two trunks.

Natural informal Sokan

Deciduous trees can be used effectively for the Sokan style. The two crowns can intermingle to form a single crown or they can be developed separately. The oval container emphasises the movement of the crowns.

Slanting Sokan

The main tree is formed in the traditional way, i.e. the first branch flows in the opposite direction to the slant. The first branch of the minor tree is leaning far forward, to receive more sunlight.

Driftwood Sokan

The dramatic effect created by jins and shari's is echoed on the minor tree, which is placed towards the back to give the necessary depth. A deep rectangular container is selected to fit the size of the trunk.

Literati Sokan

The delicate lines of these literati-styled trees are best emphasised in a traditional literati container.

116

Pierneef Sokan

The smaller tree leans away from the major tree in order to capture its share of sunlight. A deep oval container emphasises the round crowns of the style.

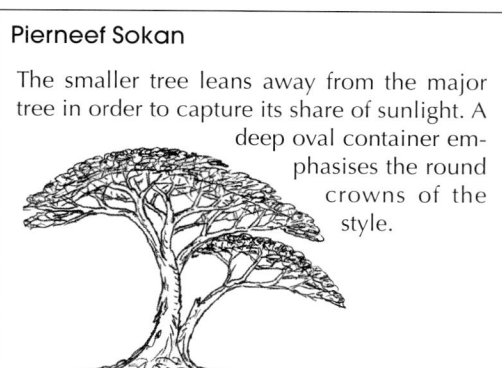

Slanting and semi-cascade Sokan

The major tree is formed into a slanting style, and keeps a watchful eye on the semi-cascading minor tree. A deep round container adds to the illusion of stability.

Windswept Sokan

The two trees echo the same mood in their struggle against the elements. To complement the creation, a flat stone is used for a natural appearance.

Root-over-rock Sokan

The two trunks flow in opposite directions and the smaller tree can easily be regarded as a major branch. A flat rectangular or oval container is ideal for this style.

Willow-style Sokan

The two trunks complement each other and form a harmonious composition. A round or oval container will complement the soft lines of this style.

Containers

As the style is usually very delicate, rectangular and oval containers can be used. Follow the same principles as for single trees with regard to choosing the depth of the pot according to trunk size. The containers shown in the sketches definitely enhance the beauty of the compositions.

Plant material

Almost any small-leafed material can be used for this style, therefore plants with compound or broad leaves should be avoided.

117

Fallen tree or raft style – Ikadabuki

The Ikadabuki style simulates a fallen tree whose upward growing branches developed into individual trees.

The fallen tree style differs from the root-connected or sinuous style (see page 121) in that the latter is more informal due to the various trunks sprouting from the main roots, whereas the fallen tree style tends to be more formal due to the upward growing branches on the trunk.

This style differs also from group plantings (see page 150) in that the latter consist of several trees with individual root systems. Note that the same rules that apply to group plantings regarding perspective, negative space, focal point and silhouette line also apply to the Ikadabuki style.

An advantage of the fallen tree style is that the plant characteristics, e.g. leaf size and autumn colours, are identical. The biggest disadvantage is that the artist cannot easily reconstruct the style due to the limitations of the branches.

This Japanese five-needle pine has been styled into the fallen tree or raft style. The original owner collected the material in the mountains. Mr Iwasaki named the tree 'Iwasaki Yatsubusa No 1' after his own name.

Guidelines for creating the fallen tree style

Formal Ikadabuki

The two strongest branches are used as the focal point and the two supporting trees of various lengths are placed close to them. On the far side, a group of tree trunks forms a smaller triangle, and also gives depth to the composition. An oval or rectangular container is recommended.

Formal group Ikadabuki

The longest and strongest branches are placed in the foreground and the smallest branches at the back, to create the correct perspective. To avoid a monotonous appearance, the trunks are placed at varying distances from each other.

Formal Ikadabuki with one dominant tree as the focal point

To create the necessary depth, do not place the trunks in a single line but place some to the front and others to the back. A shallow oval container complements the style.

Informal Ikadabuki

The original trunk is buried halfway into the ground, to suggest the fallen tree. The trees follow the same movement of the major trunk. An oval container complements the movement of the trunks.

Informal Ikadabuki with a dominant tree as focal point

The spaces between the trunks vary and it is often necessary to build up the soil level to accommodate the roots. The soil level should, however, not be too high as it would spoil the scene.

Natural Ikadabuki with two trunks

Sometimes it happens that a double-trunk tree is blown over by strong winds, and the result is that a very natural grove starts to develop. A shallow but broad oval container displays the style well.

119

Slanting Ikadabuki

For optimum effect, the various trunks flow in the same direction. To create the necessary depth, the lengths of the trunks become shorter towards the end. A shallow oval container captures the feeling of grace and elegance radiated by the composition.

Pine-shape Ikadabuki

Trees of approximately the same length form a harmonious ensemble. The small tree in the centre creates depth. A shallow oval container rounds off the peaceful setting.

Literati Ikadabuki

The literati style requires elegant and slender trees with minimal foliage. Choose either a flat stone or slate, because an oval or rectangular container would look too formal.

Dominant slanting Ikadabuki

This style simulates a scene with a big tree in the foreground and smaller trees in the distance. The individual trunks must be artistically grouped to ensure a pleasing end result.

Windswept Ikadabuki

An interesting sense of windswept trees can be created with the correct plant material – conifers are excellent for this purpose. To simulate windy conditions, the foliage should be sparse. An oval container, or flat stone or slate, will complement the style.

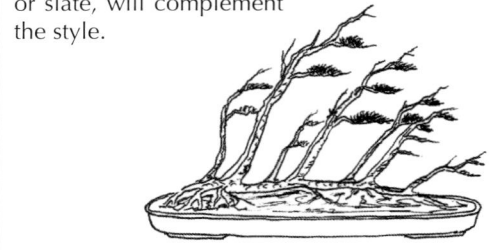

Containers

Rectangular or oval containers are usually suitable. Flat stones or slates can also be used, as the style is very natural. The container is usually shallow but the depth can vary according to the trunk's thickness.

Plant material

Conifers, *Olea*, *Podocarpus* and *Taxodium* species are ideal for the more formal Ikadabuki creations, while deciduous trees such as *Celtis*, maples, elms and other small-leafed species can be used to create a more informal effect.

120

Root-connected or sinuous style – Netsuranari

The Netsuranari style originated from a long surface root that sprouted new shoots, which grew into several trunks. The root-connected style differs from the Ikadabuki style as the latter symbolises a tree which has fallen down and of which the branches grew vertically from the fallen trunk. Hence the Netsuranari is a natural and informal style, often found in nature. As these two styles originate from a single tree, they differ from the group or forest style in which individual trees are used.

This example of the root-connected style is created by using a Japanese five-needle pine tree. Owned by the late Mr Iwasaki.

Guidelines for creating the root-connected style

Informal Netsuranari

One often finds that some trees such as elm (*Ulmus* species), hackberry or wild stinkwood (*Celtis* species), crape myrtle or pride of India (*Lagerstroemia*), wild fig (*Ficus* species), etc. send out shoots on their surface roots. These roots tend to be informal, hence the informal appearance. The general rule, however, is that trunks in group plantings should never cross.

Netsuranari with a dominant tree as the focal point

A 'close view' can be created by developing the front main tree, and by placing the smaller trees in a supporting position slightly to the back and to the sides to give the required perspective. A deep rectangular container, selected according to the thickness of the trunk, will be the right choice.

Slanting Netsuranari

All the trees are following the same trunk movement. The smaller trees are placed on the leaning side to give depth to the composition, whereas the second biggest tree is supporting the major tree. A rectangular or an oval container will complement the design.

Root-over-rock Netsuranari

It is a natural habit of most of the *Ficus* species to shoot out on the main roots, making the wild figs an excellent choice for this style. A rectangular container is ideal for this composition.

Literati Netsuranari

The various trunks have developed into delicate literati styled trees. Do not over-develop the growth, as the foliage should be sparse and well defined. The boat-shaped stone rounds off the composition.

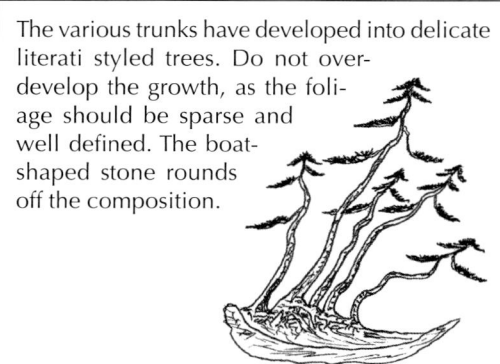

Containers

Various containers such as rectangular, oval, bowl-shaped as well as a flat stone or slate can be used for the style.

Plant material

Any small-leafed plant material is suitable. Conifers and, especially, some of the *Ficus* species are highly recommended. Also see the list of trees under *Informal Netsuranari* above.

Turtle-back or stump style – Korabuki

Although this style is found in nature, it is not a very common style and not often seen in bonsai collections.

This style is closely related to the clump style, except that the base is *swollen* like the shell of a turtle. This unusual style was inspired by the surface roots of the wild olive, wild fig and maple which sometimes develop into a bulgy base.

In the Korabuki style the number of trunks is uneven and the trunks never cross. The dominant trunk forms the focal point, and the smaller and shorter trunks support it.

This style can be artificially formed by inarching the same species through holes in the dome surface.

This beautiful Moreton Bay fig (*Ficus macrophilla*) is a fine example of the turtle-back style, created by Mr Leong Kwong from Sydney, Australia.

Guidelines for creating the turtle-back style

Triple-trunk Korabuki

The major trunk dominates the scene and the two minor trunks support the main trunk. For the best effect the tree is planted just off-centre. A deep oval-shaped container is used to suit the trunk base.

Five-trunk Korabuki

The width of the trunks is nearly the same. The trunks vary in length – the tallest trunk is regarded as the main tree and the styling of the rest is done in accordance with the main trunk. An oval container with an infold lip enhances the beauty of the creation.

Seven-trunk Korabuki

The focus here is on the base and trunk framework of this impressive tree. It is important not to cross trunks as it would mar the beauty and harmony of the composition. The deep round container matches the size of the trunk and the length of the container is equal to the width of the crown.

Containers

The selection of the correct container depends on the composition, but oval round or rectangular containers are mostly used.

Clump or sprout style – Kabudachi

The clump style is often found in nature where seeds from the same seedpod germinate to form a cluster of young plants that grow closely together. The base eventually fuses to form a tree with a single root system but with several trunks.

The sprout style can also develop where a young seedling that has been damaged sends out numerous new shoots to survive. The various trunks develop later on as single trees. To be able to receive as much sunlight as possible, the trunks grow sideways to form a beautiful multiple-trunk tree.

In bonsai the style can be imitated by planting several trunks closely together. These plants will eventually fuse to give the appearance of a multiple-trunk tree with one root system. The Kabudachi style evokes a feeling of tranquillity and may look simple to create but it is in fact a challenge to master.

This five-needle pine (*Pinus pentaphylla* var. *himekomatsu*) was carefully trained in the multiple-trunk or clump style by Mr Iwasaki.

125

Guidelines for creating the clump style

Introduction

When selecting trees for the clump style, it is important to use trees of different trunk lengths and widths.

Trees can be grouped together in numbers of three, five, seven or more. The individual trees should be well developed beforehand to speed up the overall end result.

Triple-trunk composition

There are two options open to the creator of this style:
- The major tree can be placed either in the centre or on the side.
- The minor tree can be placed in the centre.

Triple-trunk Kabudachi with the major tree in the centre

Formal Kabudachi

The major trunk is placed in the centre and the two minor trees slightly towards the front. The branch placement is the same as for a single trunk. The first branch is always placed on the smallest trunk with branches on the outside of the trunks. No branches are allowed between the trunks, and no long branches are allowed directly above the minor trunks.

Informal Kabudachi

The major tree forms the focal point of this 'close-view' composition. To create harmony and balance, the trunks follow the same movement.

Slanting Kabudachi

The length and thickness of the trunks vary to accentuate the illusion of distance. A natural stone, slate or oval container would capture the movement of this composition.

Windswept Kabudachi

The major trunk is placed slightly forward, and the second tree follows the same trunk movement. The smallest tree gives depth to the composition and fills the negative space underneath the major tree. A flat round container captures the movement of the trunks.

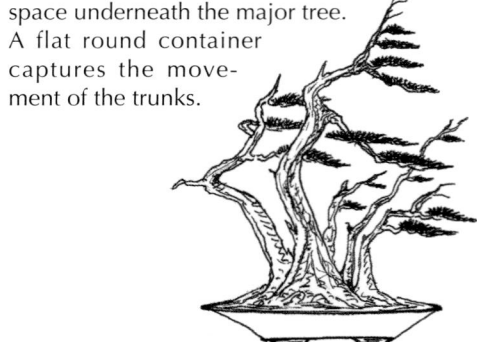

Triple-trunk Kabudachi with the apexes in different directions

The two major trunks form the focal point, and the smallest trunk is slanting in the opposite direction. It is important that the distances between the trunks should vary to give depth to the composition. For the best effect, plant the trees either in a round or an oval container.

Triple-trunk Kabudachi with the major tree on one side

The dominant tree forms the focal point, and the two smaller trees are in a supporting position. An important aspect of this style is that trunks must not cross each other. The silhouette line forms a triangle.

Deciduous Kabudachi

Although the two minor trees are planted on the same side, the major tree is the dominant feature. Remember that the trunks should be planted close to each other to simulate a single root system. The silhouette line forms a dome or an open umbrella. A deep rectangular container is used to match the trunk size.

Triple-trunk Kabudachi with the smallest tree in the centre

Slanting Kabudachi with the two minor trees slanting in opposite directions

An interesting scene can be created when the minor tree is placed in the centre. Here the two major trees are slanting sideways to accentuate the minor tree which is giving depth to the creation. The proportions between the trunks must be kept in mind, i.e. the tallest trunk should be the thickest and the shortest trunk should, therefore, be the thinnest.

Slanting Kabudachi with the trees slanting in the same direction

Perspective is created by placing the minor trunk at the back. Symmetrical designs should be avoided. A three-dimensional effect, as well as depth, can be created by an asymmetrical design. The flat stone gives a natural appearance to the creation.

FIVE-TRUNK KABUDACHI

Informal Kabudachi style – open umbrella

The same rules apply here as for the triple-trunk Kabudachi, i.e. trunks must not cross each other. The silhouette line forms a harmonious unit, and it could be triangular, dome-shaped or flame-shaped. The dominant trunk is the tallest and thickest, while the others become gradually smaller and shorter. The various crowns or apexes should be well defined.

Flame-shaped Kabudachi

The trees have a flame shape, which is normally found among deciduous trees. The smaller trunks are placed to the back to provide the necessary depth. An oval container complements the oval silhouette line.

Root-over-rock Kabudachi

Although this design reminds one of the root-connected style or Netsuranari, it is in fact a clump style over a rock. The criterion by which this style is judged is that the bonsai should consist of several trunks sprouting from the same root base.

Slanting five-trunk Kabudachi

Trunk movement is created by the slant of the trunks. The trees suggest the edge of a forest, or a windy spot at the edge of a steep cliff. An oval container accentuates the movement of the trunks.

The same variations in style can be created for the five-trunk Kabudachi as suggested for the triple-trunk Kabudachi.

Containers

Oval, rectangular, round or hexagonal containers may be used, as well as natural stone or slate. Shallow to medium-depth containers will complement this magnificent style.

Plant material

Conifers, small-leafed evergreens and deciduous plant material can be used. If separate plants are used, make sure that they are from the same mother plant.

128

Artistic styles

Literati or free style – Bunjin

Windswept style – Fuki-nagashi

Driftwood style – Shari-miki

The allure of this Japanese scarlet apricot is exemplified by the lovely blossoms. There is an old Japanese saying that states: 'Every occasion of extending hospitality to another person is a once-in-a-lifetime chance, so one should try to make each occasion perfect' – a fitting metaphor for the fleeting beauty of the blossoming flowers. Owned by the late Mr Iwasaki.

Literati or free style – Bunjin

Literati or free style is regarded as the most advanced form of bonsai and the avant-garde of all bonsai styles. The style originated in China during the Han period, as far back as AD 206. The Chinese have a far more philosophical approach towards bonsai than any other nation, therefore each creation tells a story or has a symbolic meaning.

The word 'literati' is derived from a Chinese word which describes the intellectual elite of Chinese society of the era. This group of people was skilled in the traditional arts such as philosophy, literature, music, poetry, sculpture and painting. The bonsai they created were tall and slender, and their abstract beauty could be compared with that of calligraphy. The creations exuded a total freedom of expression.

About two hundred years ago, the famous Japanese artist Hiroshige painted the first Japanese version of the literati concept. In this painting he applied his graphic technique to depict natural scenes, which also included interesting tree forms. The Japanese version of the literati style is called Bunjin.

'Literati' is regarded as the original name given to this style and as it is very descriptive, it should be used instead of other names.

True literati bonsai can only be created once all the rules of the traditional bonsai styles have been mastered. The following quotation from the *Mustard Seed Garden Manual of Painting* seems equally applicable to the creation of literati bonsai:

Among those who study painting some strive for an elaborate effect and others prefer the simple. Neither complexity in itself nor simplicity is enough. Some aim to be deft, other to be laboriously careful. Neither dexterity nor conscientiousness is enough. Some set great value on method: others pride themselves on dispensing with method. To be without method is deplorable but to depend entirely on method is worse. You must learn first to observe the rules faithfully: afterwards, modify them according to your intelligence and capacity. The end of all method is to seem to have no method.

If you aim to dispense with method, learn method. If you aim at facility, learn method. If you aim at facility, work hard. If you aim for simplicity master complexity.

Literati could be summarised as simple, elegant, stark beauty and suggestiveness. The charm of literati is brought to life only if one views it in a holistic manner.

The elegance of this Japanese red pine (*Pinus densiflora*) is captured in the literati style of its old driftwood trunk. Owned by the late Mr Iwasaki.

130

Mr Iwasaki bought this beautiful literati styled Japanese five-needle pine (*Pinus pentaphylla* var. *himekomatsu*) in remembrance of his visit to Mr Kobayashi who styled the tree.

A *Buddleja saligna* styled in the literati style by the author.

This *Buddleja saligna* was collected 1985 by the author and has been shaped into the literati style. The small accent tree is a *Ficus burtt davyi*.

Guidelines for creating the literati style

The link with nature

Trees growing in deep gorges have a tendency to grow tall and lanky in search of sunlight. Their rugged appearance is caused by debris falling from the upper cliffs. On top of the cliffs strong winds tend to blow the branches in all directions, hence the sometimes exaggerated forms of the trees.

Trunk

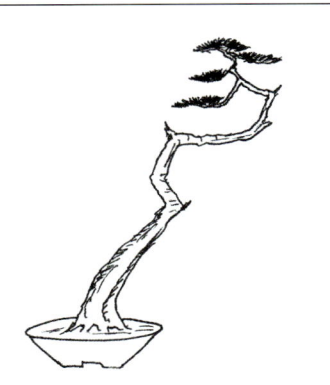

The trunk is regarded as the most important feature of the style. Although the trunk is slender, it must have strong rhythm and line movement. The curves are very prominent and the trunk must taper well towards the apex.

Trunk line movement

Single line

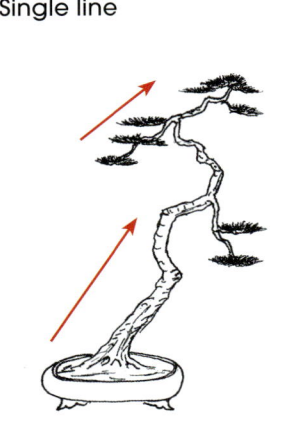

The trunk line is very simple and moves away from the base. The top portion also moves in the same direction.

Double line

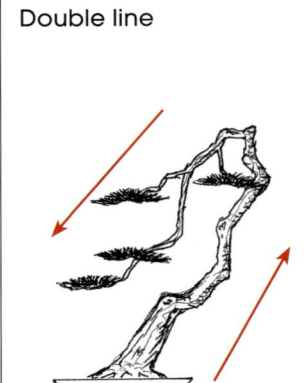

In the double-line movement the trunk first slants upwards to the right and then makes a sharp turn to the left.

Branch line movement

The following sketches illustrate single line movement with symmetrical and asymmetrical balance.

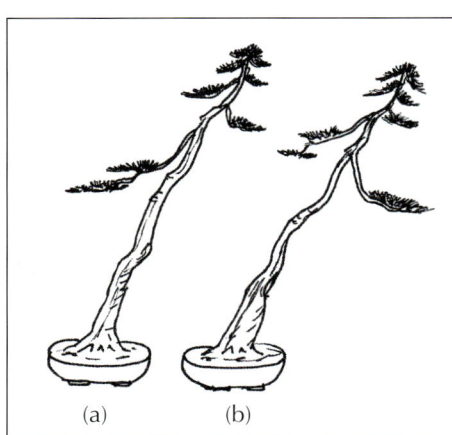

(a) Symmetrical:
If the first branch is on the opposite side of the trunk line direction, the tree is symmetrically balanced.

(b) Asymmetrical:
If the first branch is on the same side as the trunk line direction, the tree is asymmetrically balanced.

(a)   (b)

General rules

- Round containers are usually used because a literati style does not have a definite front.
- A handmade container suits the style the best.
- Not much emphasis is placed on the root system.
- Branches are few in number and not too long.
- Foliage is sparse to suggest the struggle of the tree as it is found in nature.
- Two-thirds of the trunk is normally free of branches.

Avoid bushy growth. When dense growth is allowed, the artistic impact and delicate lines of the tree are lost.

The final product after refinement has taken place. The true feeling of the literati has been revealed. Although the literati style is simple, true simplicity, plus balance and beauty, are very difficult to attain.

Possible variations for the literati style

Formal upright literati

An elegant effect is achieved with the sparse use of foliage.

Informal upright literati

The first branch has been brought forward to balance the top portion. Although this branch crosses the trunk, this is permissible in the literati style.

Slanting literati

The simplicity of line movement is the dominant characteristic of this tree. A deep round container provides the necessary stability to the creation.

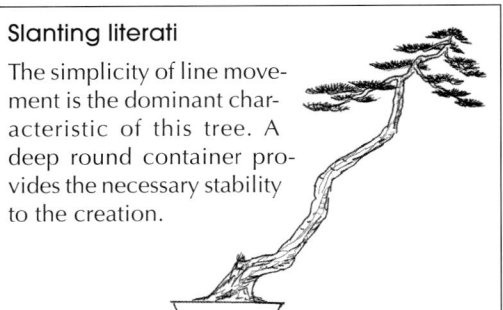

Extreme slanting literati

This artistic creation confirms the fact that the literati is the avant-garde of the bonsai styles.

Semi-cascading literati

With the triangle as the theme, movement and balance form the strong point in this design. A deep container adds to the feeling of lightness, but also provides stability.

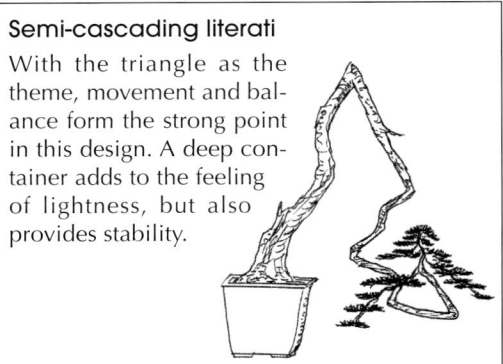

This literati exudes softness, gracefulness and a sense of continuous movement.

This semi-cascade literati is reminiscent of a yoga pose. A deep semi-cascade pot gives stability to the overhanging tree.

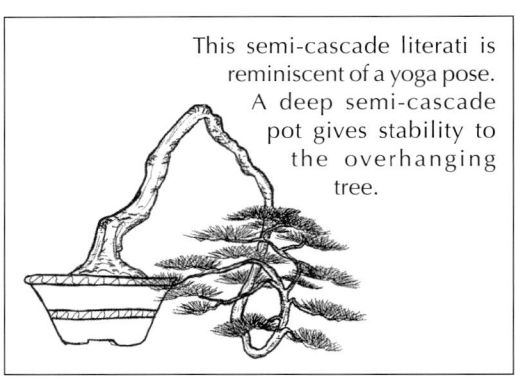

This dramatic composition simulates a tree growing on a steep cliff, in its struggle for survival.

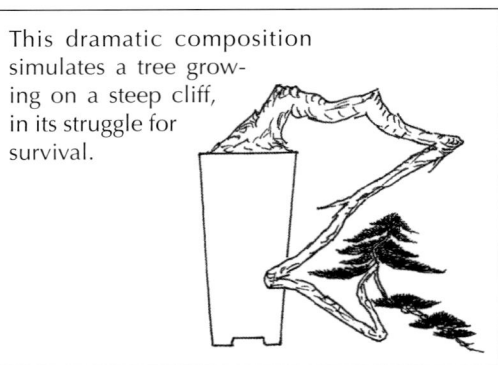

The sparse usage of foliage highlights the smooth movement line of this literati cascade.

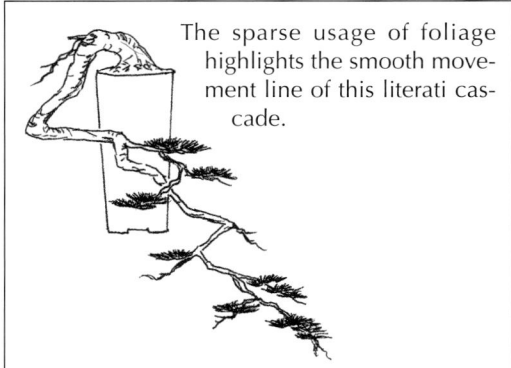

The reverse movement emphasises the anti-clockwise movement of the tree. A dish-like pot gives a feeling of lightness to the creation.

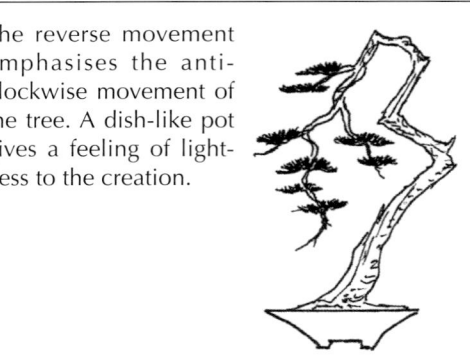

134

The tree not only has an air of fragility, but also of carefree and fluttering movement.

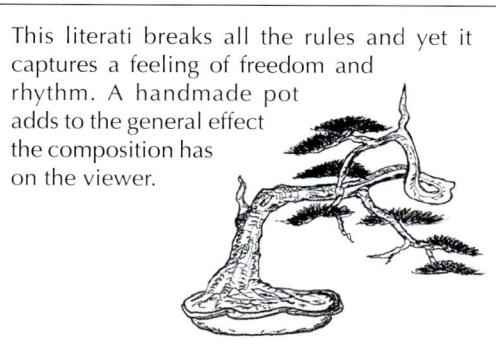

This literati breaks all the rules and yet it captures a feeling of freedom and rhythm. A handmade pot adds to the general effect the composition has on the viewer.

Hiroshige's famous painting of two delicate trees with their trunks crossed. This painting could be regarded as the inspiration for the creation of the twin-trunk literati style (see below).

This dramatic literati was initially discarded by the great bonsai master, John Naka, but saved by his wife, Alice.

Twin-trunk literati (Soju)

This composition depicts a dancing couple performing the tango. A deep dish-like container rounds off the scene.

Double-trunk literati (Sokan)

This composition depicts a happy couple. The simplicity of the design, as well as the negative space, adds to the feeling of freedom.

Triple-trunk literati (Sankan)

The smallest tree is placed at the back to create a feeling of depth. The sparse application of branches and foliage evokes the true spirit of the free style.

Korabuki literati

A feeling of rhythm and movement is captured in this multiple planting. A flat round container adds to the mood of the composition.

Yose-uye literati

Slender trees are used to simulate a young forest. Rhythm and movement form the basis of the design.

Windswept literati

The ballerina bows during her debut in Swan Lake – a feeling of graceful movement is captured in this composition.

A struggle against the forces of nature is portrayed in this windswept design.

Pierneef literati

Although slender in appearance, the raggedness of this creation tells its own story. The round container echoes the lines of the open umbrellas.

The 'Acacia' literati as seen through the eyes of the famous South African artist, Hendrik Pierneef. The painting, 'Study in Blue', captures the elegance and grace of this iconic tree of the African landscape.

The spirit of the literati

No matter by which name it is called, it remains:
- The style that is no style,
- the style that has no rules,
- the style that breaks all rules.
- It is the style you try only when you have tried all the other styles.
- It is the ultimate style ...

Containers

As indicated in the sketches, the containers must be small, and can be round, dish-like, oval or hexagonal. In the case of cascades, only delicate deep containers must be used. The reason for the small container is not only to enhance the delicate line and twig ramification of the style but also to maintain the size and form of the tree.

Plant material

Trees most commonly used are conifers and pines. Trees with small leaves and needles can be used, but trees with big flowers and plants with elaborate foliage must be avoided. Trees with slow-growing habits are best in order to keep the trunks thin and delicate.

137

Windswept style – Fuki-nagashi

This folk song from the Cape Verde Islands reminds us of the desolation embodied in the windswept style. In the windswept style, one is intensely aware of the dramatic interchange between the tree and the force of the wind. Trunks and branches are blasted aside and the jins and shari's are the silent evidence of the onslaught.

Movement is one of the most important aspects of the style and one should always be able to hear the wind blowing through the needles.

A fine example of the windswept style, this *Celtis sinensis* was created by Robert Steven of Indonesia.

Guidelines for creating the windswept style

Roots

Due to the forces of the wind, the roots on the windward side anchor the tree, and the roots on the leaning side support the trunk. There is therefore a tension on the anchoring side and a compression on the leaning side of the trunk.

Branches

Branches, as well as the foliage, are sparse to emphasise the effect of the prevailing winds.

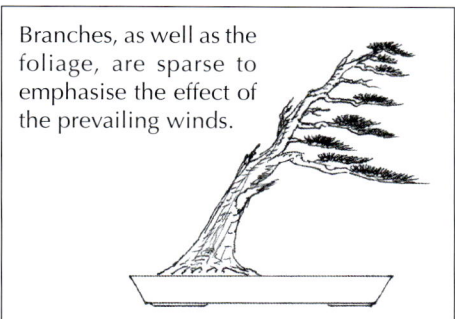

To create a feeling of depth, it is important to have back branches. As a limited number of branches are allowed, the tree can easily adopt a fan shape without the essential back branches.

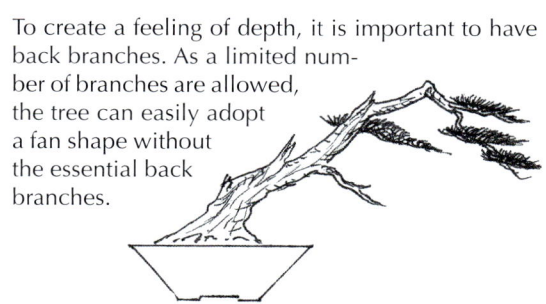

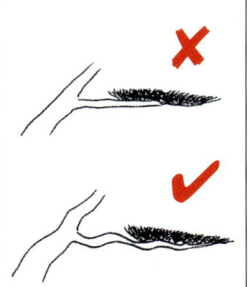

Branches are curved and not straight to emphasise the feeling of movement.

As in the literati style, major branches may cross the trunk line, but make sure that it does not look artificial. Try to avoid half-moon branches.

Jins usually occur on branches that extend into the wind. Shari's (strips of peeled bark) are often seen on the windward side of the tree.

Branches on the windward side tend to be shorter than those on the sheltered side. Do not allow the foliage to become bushy and lush; keep it trimmed.

The branches are broken due to strong winds. In this manner jins are formed.

Branch placement

The conventional branch placement – termed the 'group of three branches' – is well suited to this style. The number of branch groupings though, depends on the length of the trunk. An average tree of 30 cm may have a total of three groupings.

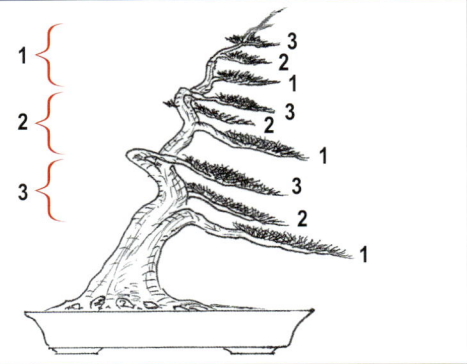

Basic windswept styles

The effect of the wind is evident in the following basic styles.

Formal upright windswept

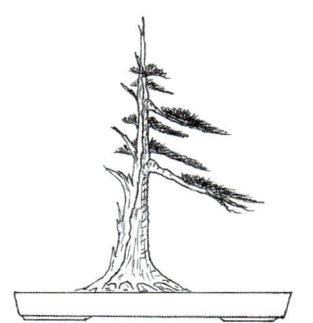

The branches on the windward side are torn off by strong winds.

Informal upright windswept

Although the tree has an informal appearance, the effect of the wind is noticeable in the flow of the branches.

Slanting windswept (Shakan)

Because of constant winds, the tree is forced to grow into a slanting position.

Extreme slanting windswept

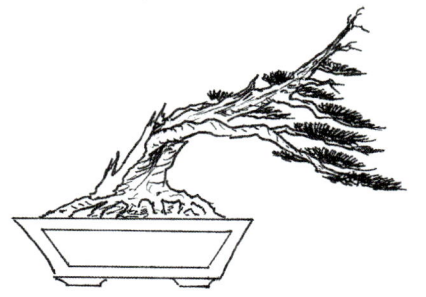

Although it may seem as if the wind is going to uproot the tree, a sense of strength and endurance is captured in this creation.

Two-line semi-cascade windswept

The compact container gives stability to this interesting windswept style.

Single-line semi-cascade windswept

The plain deep round container highlights the drama of this design.

Double-trunk windswept (Sokan)

A feeling of naturalness is captured in this design and is achieved by using a natural stone as container. A flat slate will also serve the purpose.

Triple-trunk windswept (Sankan)

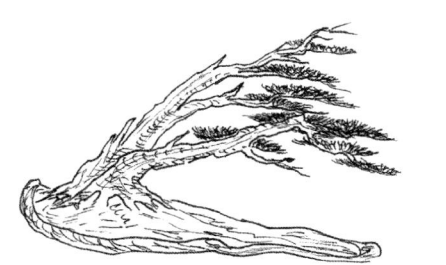

The repetition and rhythm of the branches create an illusion of trees constantly buffeted by windstorms.

A group of windswept trees (Yose-uye)

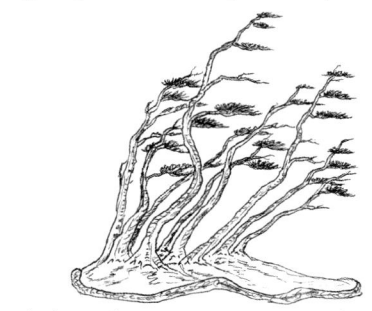

A feeling of movement is captured in this group planting.

Negative space

Negative space plays an important role in the creation of a windswept effect.

This literati styled windswept tree is a classic example of the use of negative space, which in this case is a positive feature. A bowl-shaped container emphasises the slender trunk and the movement of the branches.

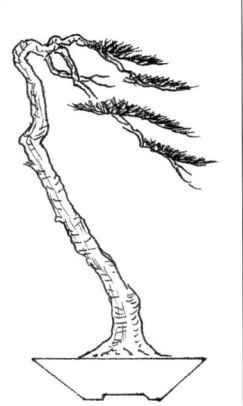

This literati styled tree imparts a feeling of struggle for survival against the harsh elements of nature. A round drum-shaped pot draws attention to the dramatic effect of this design.

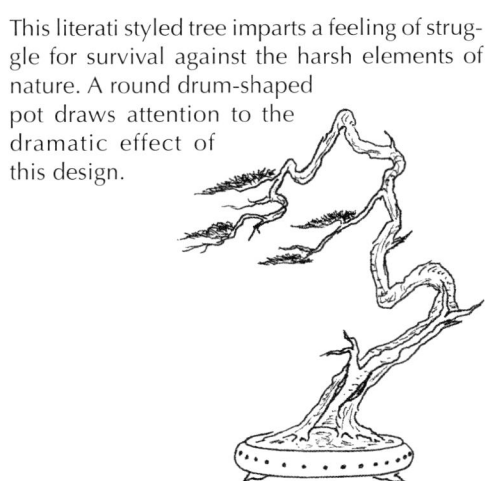

A prime example of the windswept style, this Japanese five-needle pine (*Pinus pentaphylla* var. *himeko-matsu*) captures the struggle of a tree fighting against the elements of nature. The tree belonged to the late Mr Iwasaki.

How nature creates windswept styles

On high mountains, it is not unusual to find a trunk leaning into the wind. It is due to the formation of dry air cells on the windward side and the overdevelopment of air cells on the leeward side. This has a curvature effect on the trunk. The strong winds blowing over the cliff, force the top part of the tree in the opposite direction to create an attractive windswept style as shown in the sketch.

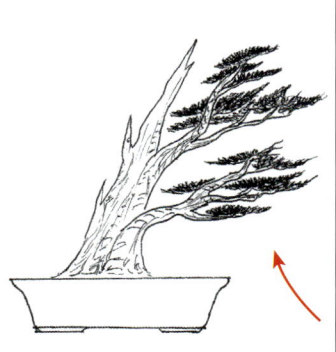

Air currents rising from below tend to blow the main branches upward against the trunk. In this way another interesting windswept effect is created.

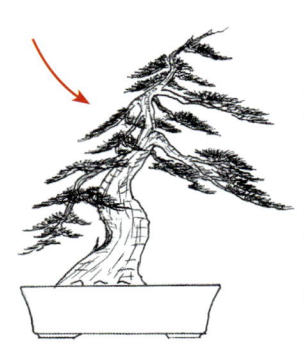

Winds blowing down a gorge force the side branches against the trunk.

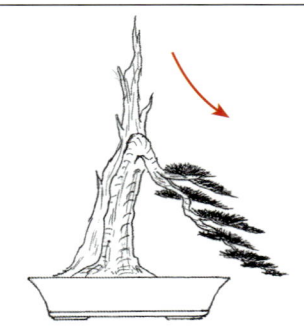

The sketch shows an old tree that endures constant winds and snow. Only one branch is left as a reminder of the relentless forces of nature. The deep pot complements the size of the weathered trunk.

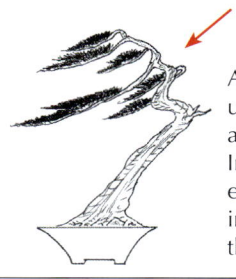

A tree near the top of a cliff tends to grow upright. Prevailing winds blowing from above force the top branches downwards. In this composition, the branch placement echoes the rhythm and feeling of the buffeting elements. A bowl-shaped pot reinforces the feeling of movement.

Seasonal winds blowing from one direction in summer and the opposite direction in winter resulted in the sparse foliage and the twisted appearance of the trunk.

A medium strong wind, blowing upwards from the gorge, caused the top branches to grow in an upward direction, while the branch development on the leeside of the wind remains fairly normal. Consequently, an interesting three-trunk, root-over-rock, semi-windswept style has been created.

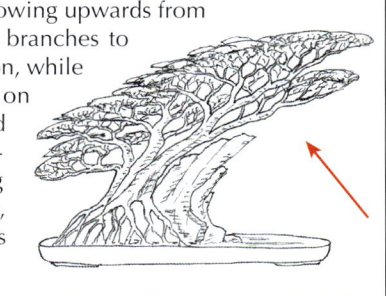

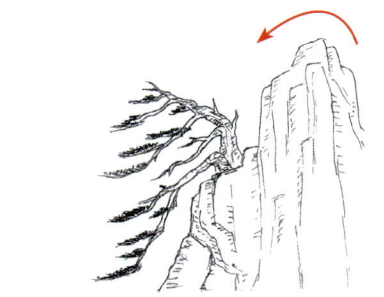

Constant winds blowing over the edge of the cliff force the tree downwards, from a semi-cascade into a full cascade style.

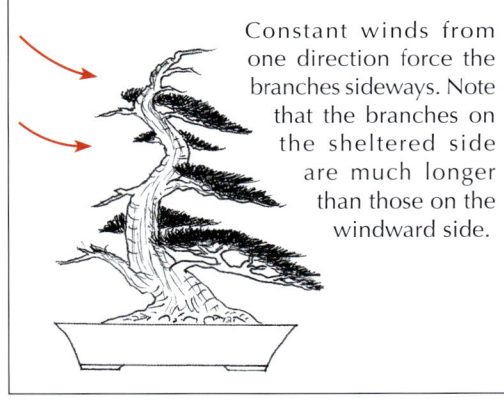

Constant winds from one direction force the branches sideways. Note that the branches on the sheltered side are much longer than those on the windward side.

Twin trunk (Soju)

Jins are the result of a constant battering of sand against the trunks. Since the wind blows from the top, all the apexes are jinned.

Triple trunk (Sankan)

The tree in the sketch has been buffeted by strong winds over a lengthy period with the result that the main branches have died. The branches on the sheltered side, though, are still battling for survival against the onslaught.

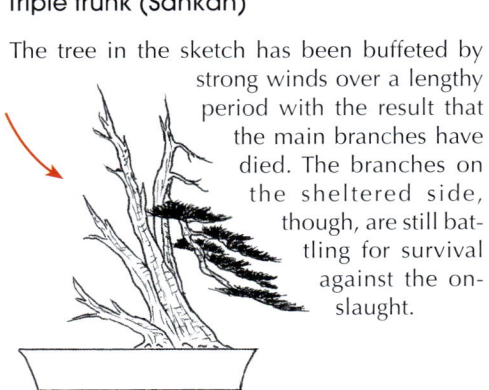

This is an outstanding example of the dramatic mood of nature, designed by Robert Steven.

The following sketches illustrate the effect of wind on the shape of the tree.

This sketch shows the basic slanting bonsai without any wind blowing.

A strong wind blowing the sub-branches and twigs upward.

A gentle wind blowing which is not strong enough to move the branches.

A windswept slanting style formed as a result of prevailing winds.

HAIKU

Morning sun is shining on the shoulders,
Autumn wind is blowing through the hair,
Although the whisper has no colours,
Yet the rhythm is there ...

Robert Steven

144

Common mistakes

A typical windswept atmosphere is lacking in these creations:

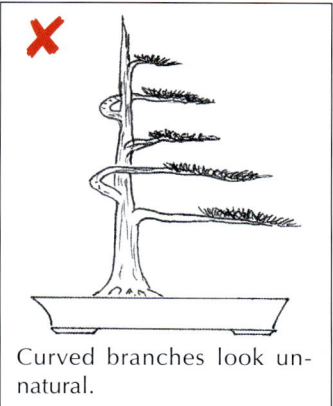

Curved branches look un-natural.

A tree with a straight trunk looks unnatural.

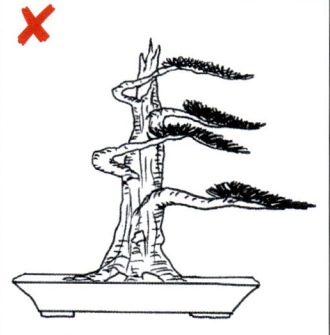

A robust tree with an aged trunk does not suit the style.

Remember

- A formal, upright tree trunk is seldom found in windy regions.
- Branches curving around the tree trunk look unnatural.
- A straight trunk with only the top branches bending in the direction of the wind looks artificial.
- It is not possible to create a windswept atmosphere with vertical side branches.
- To depict the movement of constant winds, the branches should point in the direction the wind blows and not the other way round.

Containers

As shown in the sketches, containers play a vital role in creating a feeling of movement and rhythm. Containers that are suitable for the literati style are usually also suitable for the windswept style.

Containers with wide outer lips are recommended, as they contribute towards a feeling of movement. Oval containers are ideal for emphasising movement and rhythm. To accentuate movement, the tree is usually planted on the windward side of the container.

Plant material

Conifers, pines and small-leafed evergreen plants are ideal for creating windswept styles. Plants with lush foliage are unsuitable, because the final impression should be one of a tree battling against the elements of nature. Deciduous trees may also be used and are especially impressive in winter. Although deciduous trees do not normally grow at high altitudes, they do occur in areas such as Indonesia and Malaysia where constant winds are blowing.

A final thought on the windswept style from Deborah R. Koreshoff:

The wind-swept tree tells us its tale clearly and dramatically. We can almost feel the wind and hear its melancholy song, and, if there is balance and grace, we are left with the sense that there is much more to life than to merely survive.

Driftwood style – Shari-miki

Bonsai is an art form of which the sculpturing aspect requires a great deal of skill and creativity. The bonsai master is, in fact, creating a living sculpture. This is especially so when working in the driftwood style, as driftwood has a mystic beauty and a distinctive framework that few other styles have.

Most styles are suited to the driftwood approach because it is not bound to a particular style or shape and, furthermore, not much effort is required to turn deadwood into a driftwood design. There are, however, exceptions – the broom, baobab, Pierneef, willow and other distinctive, well-defined styles do not lend themselves to the driftwood style.

Driftwood has a dramatic impact on the tree and likewise on the viewer, and its main function is to lend a certain artistic appeal to the design.

The driftwood phenomenon is found at high altitudes where plants have to battle against the elements for survival. To illustrate: a tree has to withstand constant attacks of prevailing winds, snowstorms, scourging desert winds as well as sandblasts, which usually leave only a narrow strip of bark on which the tree is dependent for its survival.

The end result should always reflect a tree with character. It is imperative that the attention of the artist is focused on the dramatic aspects of the driftwood style, as the following sketches will illustrate.

A superb example of the driftwood style, this Shimpaku juniper was refined by the famous Mr Masahiko Kimura. The tree belonged to the late Mr Iwasaki.

Guidelines for creating the driftwood style

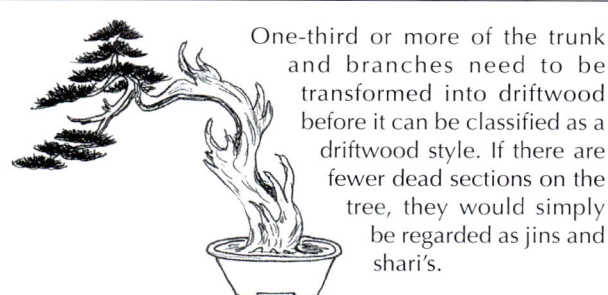

One-third or more of the trunk and branches need to be transformed into driftwood before it can be classified as a driftwood style. If there are fewer dead sections on the tree, they would simply be regarded as jins and shari's.

As previously mentioned, the driftwood effect is too dramatic for it to be incorporated into well-defined and delicate styles such as the broom, baobab, Pierneef, willow and other styles. To create an illusion of struggle and suffering, keep the foliage sparse, because dense growth does not enhance the dramatic effect which the artist is striving for.

The driftwood (jins) and the peeled bark (shari's) are both important features of the style. Take care not to create driftwood during the inactive season as it could lead to the disintegration of the root system with devastating results for the tree.

Famous driftwood styles

'Grass on the roadside' is the poetic name given to this masterpiece. This tree, a Shimpaku juniper, is also the logo of the Bonsai Society of Greater New York, Inc.

'Tora' or 'Tiger' is the poetic name given to this tree by the world-famous and beloved Master of Bonsai, John Naka. This California juniper, in typical driftwood style, was collected in 1962, the year of the tiger. The tree has a strong trunk base and to create this magnificent driftwood style, most of the bark has been sandblasted to reveal a beautiful bare trunk.

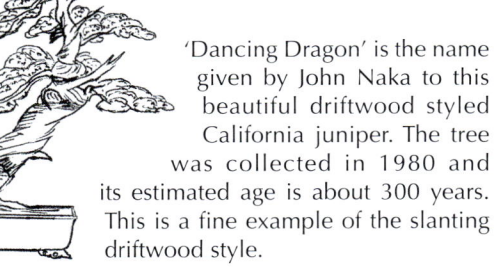

'Dancing Dragon' is the name given by John Naka to this beautiful driftwood styled California juniper. The tree was collected in 1980 and its estimated age is about 300 years. This is a fine example of the slanting driftwood style.

Another dramatic California juniper, belonging to Tatsu Yago of the California Bonsai Society. The tree resembles a camel on its journey through the desert. Only a strip of live bark keeps the tree alive.

Another slanting driftwood style: note that the first branch is slanting against the movement of the trunk. This beautiful California juniper belongs to Ernie Kuo of California.

This literati driftwood belongs to Warren Hill of California and was collected in the mountains of California. The California juniper, with its hard wood, is excellent material for the driftwood style. Many of the California junipers facing the prevailing desert winds become sandblasted.

A dramatic driftwood, sculptured by the renowned Japanese Master, Masahiko Kimura. Mr Kimura is often referred to as the 'Magician' because of his extraordinary talent for bonsai sculpture. His great skill at transforming ordinary bonsai into masterpieces is quite awe-inspiring. He collected this Shimpaku juniper in the Itoigawa river area in Japan.

A Shimpaku juniper, refined by Masahiko Kimura. The dramatic sculpturing of the driftwood portion transforms this tree into a masterpiece. Note the interesting rectangular pot with its overlip and round corners, which emphasise the movement of the tree.

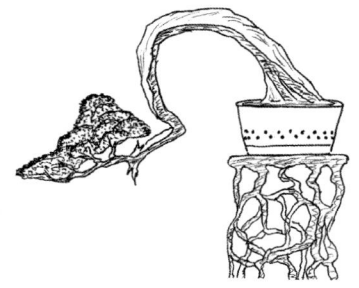

A semi-cascade driftwood style, this California juniper was collected in 1978 and trained by John Naka. Note how the drum-shaped container emphasises the trunk movement. The carefully selected stand displays this dramatic tree to great effect. The dark strip is the bark section, which contains cambium that keeps the tree alive. It blends in well with the stand, which is made from tree roots.

A *Buddleja saligna* designed in the driftwood style by the author. Height: 90 cm.

Containers

Like the gilded frames of paintings by the Old Masters such as Rembrandt and other Renaissance artists, containers should be chosen to emphasise the dramatic effect presented by a driftwood sculpture. Depending on the movement captured in a sculpture, the container could be oval, hexagonal, rectangular or bowl-shaped. As the mood of the design determines the shape of the container, you should make a thorough study of the containers used by the great masters (see the sketches in this section) to help you develop a feel for the right container.

Plant material

Only hardwood evergreens with small leaves are suitable for the driftwood style; therefore conifers are highly recommended, especially the *Juniper* species. Local small-leafed hardwood species, such as the wild olive (*Olea*), *Buddleja*, etc., are also suitable plant material. Deciduous trees – whether broad-leafed or compact-leafed – are unsuitable, because they do not usually grow at high altitudes and will therefore not withstand the fury of the elements. Hardwood trees not only last longer but also resist decay better than softwood materials.

149

Group plantings

Twin-trunk style – Soju

Triple-trunk style – Sankan

Forest plantings – Yose-uye

'Sunrise in the forest', recipient of a golden award at the 2006 Chinese Penjing Competition. This dramatic forest planting of a large group of *Celtis sinensis* trees, was designed by the author (see also page 167).

Twin-trunk style – Soju

In the twin-trunk style each tree has its own root system, in contrast with the Sokan style where the two trees share the same root system.

The two trees bring to mind a relationship between two people: perhaps a couple, two close friends, or even a grandparent and grandchild. Hence the main objective of this style is to give an illusion of unity, balance and harmony.

Deborah Koreshoff relates a fascinating Chinese tale in her book *Bonsai, its Art, Science, History and Philosophy*. According to her, if the larger tree is planted first there is a tendency to plant the smaller tree close to the larger tree as if the younger tree is supporting the older one. If the younger tree is planted first, the older tree is planted further away as if the younger tree is leading the older one. Whatever the mood one intends to convey, one should aim for complete harmony between the two trees.

Although it is better to use the same plant species from a horticultural point of view, two different tree species may also be used if their growing requirements are the same.

This five-needle pine suggests a married couple. It was part of the late Mr Iwasaki's collection.

Guidelines for creating the twin-trunk style

Trunk size

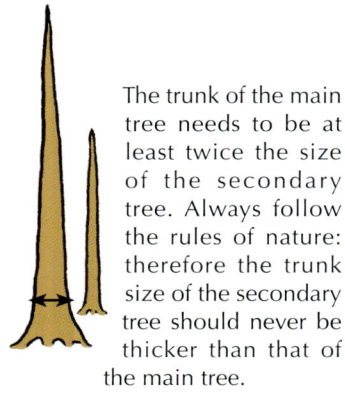

The trunk of the main tree needs to be at least twice the size of the secondary tree. Always follow the rules of nature: therefore the trunk size of the secondary tree should never be thicker than that of the main tree.

Height of the tree

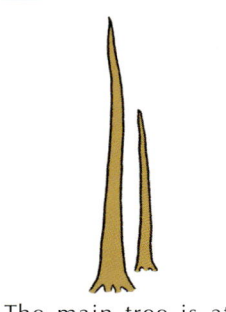

The main tree is at least one-third taller than the secondary tree.

Adjusting the height

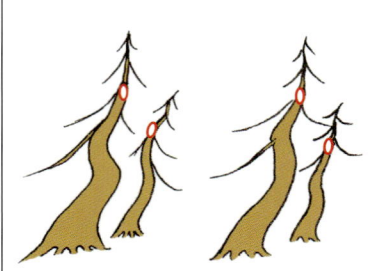

When correcting the height of two trees, it is better to have the scars facing each other, or have them pointing in the same direction.

Harmony and trunk movement

For the best harmonious effect, the trunks should follow the same trunk movement.

However, if the trunks move in opposite directions, the apexes should at least follow the same direction.

Positioning the tree

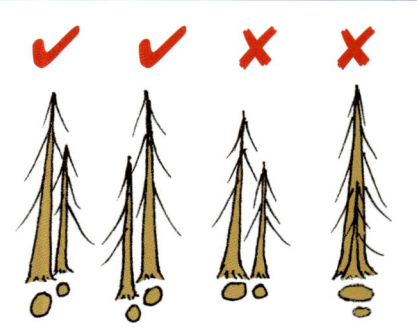

Plant the two trees in a slightly diagonal position. It does not matter which one is planted in front, as both compositions create depth, i.e. the 'grandfather' could either lead or follow. Do not plant the two trees in front of each other or next to each other.

Branch arrangement

The branch arrangement of the twin-trunk is the same as for a single tree. Therefore do not allow the branches to cross the trunks or to be on the same level.

The lowest branch is always on the smaller tree. Do not place a branch of the taller tree directly over the apex of the smaller tree, because it not only looks unnatural but also causes the apex of the smaller tree to grow sideways in search of light.

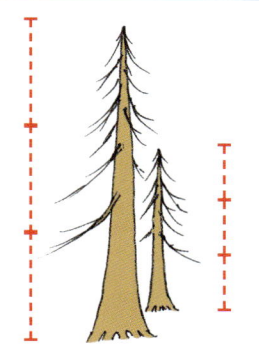

The first third of the trunks of both trees should be free of branches.

The silhouette line could be in the shape of a triangle, a ball, an umbrella or an egg.

Possible Soju styles

Formal Soju

The branches of young trees may point upwards and those of older trees may drop sharply. Note the position of the branches. This arrangement creates the illusion of a single tree. Rectangular containers are normally used for formal compositions.

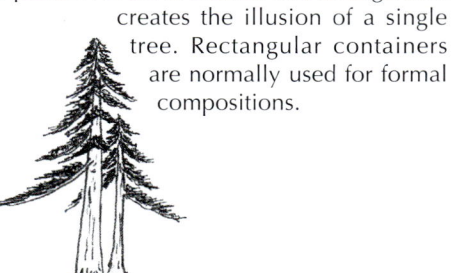

Informal Soju

The two trees form a harmonious unit even though the smaller tree leans slightly to the left, in search of sunlight. Oval or rectangular containers are suitable for this style.

Natural informal Soju

The two crowns are growing in slightly different directions, although the two trunks slant in the same direction. The silhouette line of the two trees forms a soft triangle. The oval container emphasises the gentle lines of the style.

Slanting Soju

The secondary tree is placed at the back of the main tree to give a sense of depth to the composition. Oval or rectangular containers are suitable for this style.

Slanting and semi-cascade Soju

The scene suggests two trees growing at the edge of a steep cliff, with the dominant tree keeping a watchful eye over the minor tree. Note that the cascading tree is positioned slightly nearer to the front of the container. A deep round container is recommended for this composition.

Literati Soju

The trunk line and apex follow the same movement. Keep the foliage sparse in order to emphasise the delicate trunk lines. A flat rock, or a slate, can be used very effectively as a container for this design.

Windswept Soju

A feeling of desolation is captured in these windswept trees. This feeling would, however, be lost should a formal container be used. Slate, or natural stone, is therefore the answer.

Driftwood Soju

The sketch depicts driftwood trees growing on a high mountain. The driftwood effect, created in the space between the two trees, forms the focal point. Sparse foliage emphasises the struggle for survival. A formal rectangular container rounds off the composition.

Flat-top Soju

Although the younger tree leans slightly to the right, it still gives the impression of supporting the older tree. The oval container captures the oval lines of the two apexes.

Baobab Soju

The main tree forms the focal point. The secondary tree, on the other hand, seems a long distance away. A deep rectangular container matches the trunk size, thereby creating an effect of stability.

Willow Soju

This setting radiates peace and tranquillity, because the two trees complement each other, and the trunk lines are in total harmony. Oval or round containers suit this style.

Pierneef Soju

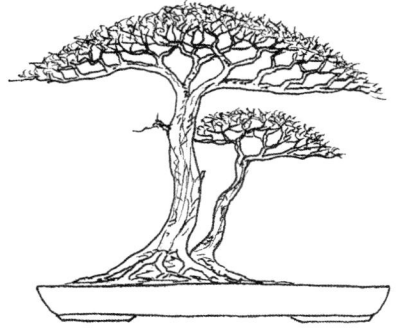

The two African thorn trees in this Pierneef Soju are growing on a savanna; perhaps giving shelter and shade to a weary pride of lions! To complement the umbrella crowns, use either an oval or a round container.

Containers

To give the required proportion to the composition, long, shallow, rectangular or oval containers are recommended. The depth of the container will depend on the trunk size.

Triple-trunk style – Sankan

In nature, the triple-trunk style is usually found at the edge of a forest.
When you position the three trees, make sure that the main tree forms the focal point.
You may place the main tree either in the middle or on the side of the arrangement.
For the best effect, use trees of the same species.

An outstanding example of a triple-trunk style. (Photograph used with permission of Nippon Bonsai Association.)

Guidelines for creating the triple-trunk style

Main tree in the centre

Informal Sankan

In the final composition one should always aim for a triangle or an umbrella silhouette. Although the hexagonal pot gives stability to the composition, it is also delicate enough to ensure an airy feeling.

Informal and slanting combination

Here the focus is on the two smaller trees which support the main tree. The oval container accentuates the movement of the trunks.

Slanting Sankan

Note that the two minor trees are planted slightly to the back. A natural stone or oval container will accentuate the movement and the mood of the composition.

Slanting and semi-cascade combination

When combining the slanting and semi-cascade styles, use a deep round container in order to suggest the edge of a cliff.

Windswept Sankan

The varying lengths of the trunks give perspective to the composition. The natural stone suggests a mountain, or a coastal scene.

Literati Sankan

In the literati style the artist may use crossed tree trunks, as this way of expressing movement and feeling is synonymous with a free and individualistic approach. A traditional dish-like container gives an airy feeling to the composition.

Apexes facing in different directions

The two supporting trees are growing slightly away from the main tree. Use a hexagonal, or literati, container when you plant the trunks closely together.

The minor tree on the right may be seen as a side branch that is following the flow of the main tree. The supporting tree on the left rounds off the scene. The oval container is a suitable choice.

The two trees slanting in the same direction can be regarded as twin trunks, while the third tree on the opposite side balances the composition. A stone, or slate, is recommended for a natural appearance.

Main tree planted on one side of the container

Apexes facing in the same direction

When the minor trees tend to slant in the same direction as the main apex, the style of the main tree can be informal.

Slanting Sankan

The angles at which the minor trees are slanting are of great importance, as they accentuate the movement of the trunk. A flat dish-like container complements the style.

The main tree forms the focal point, whereas the minor trees have a supporting function. A flat stone, or a slate, enhances the natural effect of the style.

158

Pierneef Sankan

The tree at the back gives depth to the creation. Note the rhythm and movement of the trees.

Apexes facing in different directions

In the sketch the supporting minor trees are growing in opposite directions, but the main tree still forms the focal point. The depth of the container is determined by the thickness of the main trunk.

Delicate literati trees growing on a hilltop

Depth is created by placing the smallest tree in the centre. The traditional literati pot gives stability to the delicate trees.

Containers

Round dish-like containers, hexagonal or oval containers, natural stone or slate all complement triple-trunk arrangements.

Forest plantings – Yose-uye

A well-composed forest should be able to conjure up images of birds singing, the smell of fermented leaves, fairy-painted mushrooms, the rustling of pine needles, deer darting among the shadows and the ripple of trout streams. A forest planting must have character and should exude an atmosphere of mystery, where the gazing eyes of bush babies and deer are forever alert to the threats of the jungle, where the seasons slowly change and where the interplay of dusk and dawn, sunlight, rain and dew add to the ever-changing mood of the forest.

A wide variety of scenery can be portrayed: think of the dense Knysna forest where the mysterious Knysna elephant roams, the wind-battered coastal forests of the Cape Peninsula, groves of wild olives in the Magaliesberg mountains, clusters of thorn trees in the African Bushveld, the majestic redwoods of Yosemite, and the Blackwood or Bavarian Forests in Germany, to name but a few examples.

One can compare a forest planting with a work of fine art. The bonsai artist must pay the same amount of attention to composition, structure and texture that an accomplished artist would pay to a painting or sculpture.

Deborah Koreshoff sums up the fascination of forest plantings in her book, *Bonsai its Art, Science, History and Philosophy*, as follows: 'Group settings hold a special fascination in Bonsai Art. Throughout the history of storytelling the Forest or Woodland is a place where one can go when wanting to be alone, it is a place of refuge – not unlike the church, and, in the religious sense, it can make us feel humble and, in so doing uplift the spirit. Magic and enchantment abound there and, at every turn a new adventure is born. We are drawn into the mysterious depths as if entering another world and in the dark shadows dragons dream of long forgotten secrets …'

A *Zelkova* group showing off their beautiful autumn colours. Styled by the author.

This artistically designed group of wild olive trees (*Olea europaea* subsp. *africana*) contains all the elements of harmony, depth and rhythm. Planted in 1974 and styled by the late Theuns Roos, this elegant group planting was placed among the first ten of the hundred best trees in the world by Nippon Bonsai Society in 2001. Height 30 cm. Container length 80 cm.

/8

The same group planting 25 years later under the masterful guidance of Erika Köhler.

Guidelines for creating forest plantings

When compiling a group planting of five, seven, nine, eleven or thirteen trees – or a small forest – the basic principle is that the group should consist of an uneven number of trees. When compiling bigger groups or forests, it does not matter whether one uses even or uneven numbers. A big group, for example, can consist of 30, 40, 50 or more trees.

Branch arrangement

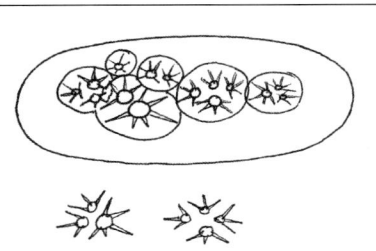

Viewed from above, the branch arrangement of a forest plantation should resemble that of a single tree, i.e. all the branches must point outwards.

The outside branches form the silhouette. Trees that are densely branched on one side are usually placed on the outside of the arrangement.

Focal point

The trunks form the focal point and are therefore one of the important features of the Yose-uye style.

In this group a single main tree forms the focal point, while the rest of the trees form the background.

The largest tree in the forest planting forms the focal point.

This sketch shows a group with various plant units and several focal points.

A strong focal point can also be created by spacing the supporting trees closely round the largest tree. This principle could also be used when a tree with a thick trunk is not available.

Note that the focal point is usually on the side with the least negative space.

Negative space

Negative space, or open areas, is an important element in creating distance and depth in a composition.

The side with the smallest trees ought to have more negative space.

Do not divide the container exactly in half, as it could result in a symmetrical design which looks unnatural in a group or forest planting.

A group planting that fills the entire container will lack balance and harmony.

To accentuate the dominant side, vary the shape and size of the negative space on each side.

Silhouette

Forest or group plantings are viewed in totality, and the silhouette is regarded as one of the most important features of the style.

The dominant tree forms the terminal point of the silhouette.

For the best visual effect, a group planting should have different-sized silhouette lines.

The lower line of the silhouette should not be straight, as straight lines result in a flat appearance, i.e. the design lacks perspective. This line normally creates a feeling of depth.

To create a feeling of movement and a sense of depth the lower line of the silhouette must curve.

Tall trunks give a captivating effect to a group planting, because the parallel vertical lines created by the trunks, draw the eye into the group.

Movement and direction

Trees should be selected and positioned in such a way that movement and direction are in harmony.

Movement can be created by positioning the group with the greater number of trees on one side of the container. This is then called the dominant side or the side with the greatest visual weight.

If the focal point is on the left side, the eye movement is from left to right, and vice versa.

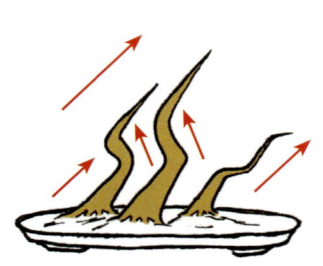

The same trunk and branch lines should be repeated throughout the composition.

164

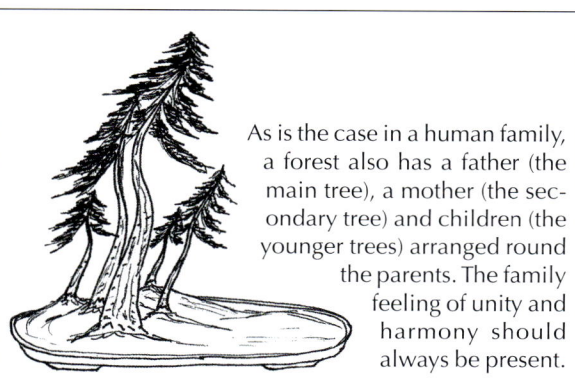

As is the case in a human family, a forest also has a father (the main tree), a mother (the secondary tree) and children (the younger trees) arranged round the parents. The family feeling of unity and harmony should always be present.

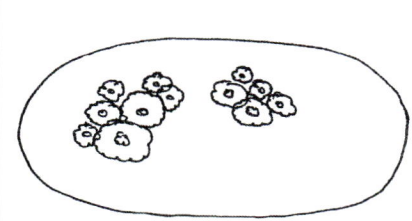

When two family units are grouped together, the dominant unit is always used as the focal point.

The art of positioning

One of the greatest challenges with forest plantings is to capture the atmosphere of a forest. One of the principal aims is to create an illusion of space and depth.

Close-up view

To create an illusion of nearness, the taller trees must be placed at the back and the smaller ones in the foreground, as illustrated here.

Perspective view

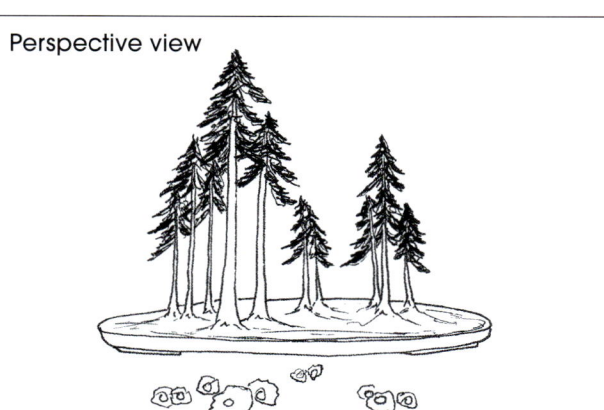

It is quite easy to create a perspective view in forest plantings as these compositions are three-dimensional: they have length, depth (width) and height. Therefore simply place the heaviest or largest trees towards the front half of the container, and plant trees that decrease progressively in height, towards the back. Well-formed trees are normally used to create this effect.

165

Distant view

In the distant view concept, the emphasis falls on the silhouette rather than on the individual tree.

To create an illusion of distance, position a smaller group of trees towards the back and on the opposite side of the main group. The diagonal line thus formed strengthens this illusion.

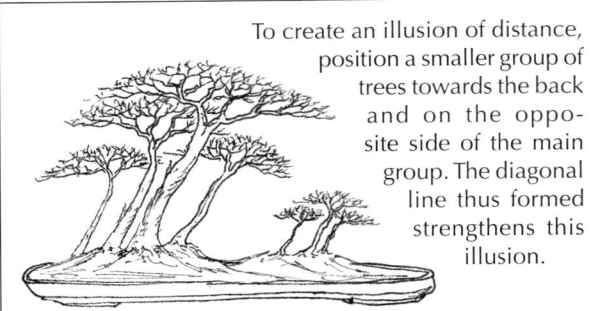

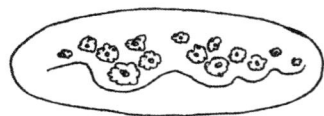

Do not plant the trees in straight lines but rather contour them in gentle curves.

Various forest styles

Formal forest

A group of tall upright trees suggests a dense forest or a close-up view arrangement.

A group of young upright trees suggests a distant view. In the sketch, trees of virtually the same size and species have been planted closely together to create a distant-view appearance.

Informal pine-shaped group

The main trees are placed in a central position whereas the smaller trees are placed in a supporting position.

Informal deciduous group

The focal point is placed on the one side of the container and enough negative space is created to the left to create an illusion of depth and vastness.

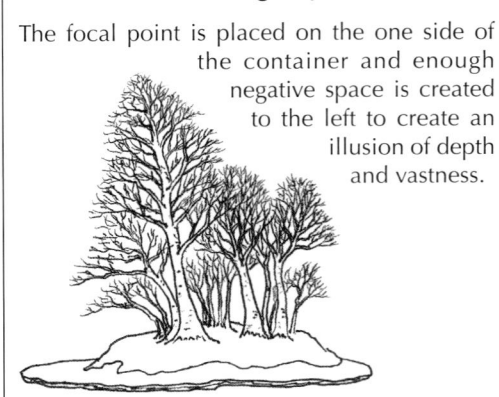

A forest of 53 hackberry trees (*Celtis sinensis*) in their summer foliage (left) and winter starkness (below), styled by the author. The trees are between 10 and 40 years old. The container is 120 cm long and the tallest tree is 50 cm high. (Photo by Sjoerd Knibbeler and Rob Wetzer.)

Slanting group

The dominant trees are placed on the left side, leaning towards the smaller trees.

Windswept group

The smaller trees are planted on the right to suggest depth. A slate is used to suggest an inhospitable environment.

Literati group

An airy feeling is created by planting the delicate literati trunks closely together. A dish-like literati container should be used for this style.

Flame group

A small tree is placed in the centre towards the back of the two families to create depth. To accentuate the formal lines of the flame style forest, a formal oval container is recommended.

Pierneef group

Two dominant focal points are created in this natural scene. A flat stone or a piece of slate may be used as a container.

Containers

Shallow containers are recommended for group settings as they reinforce the illusion of space and expanse.

Both oval and rectangular containers can be used for forest plantings. However, oval containers are preferred as the artist is not restricted to corners. Balance and an illusion of distance are therefore maintained. Flattish stones or slate also make excellent containers.

The general rule, i.e. that the trunk size must be equal to the depth of the container, is particularly applicable to forest plantings.

Plant material

Plants used for group plantings generally should:
- be hardy and able to withstand drastic pruning, training and transplanting
- have small leaves or short needles.

When different plant species are used together, select trees with similar growing habits. Most conifer species could be mixed successfully. Deciduous trees such as elms, maples, *Zelkova*, *Celtis*, etc., may also be mixed. The same rule applies to most of the thorn trees (*Senegalia / Vachellia* species; previously *Acacia* species).

When using the same plant species, select plants from the same mother plant in order to obtain similar growing characteristics, such as leaf size, autumn colouring, sprouting time, etc. Some popular species used for forest plantings are junipers, ezo spruce, *Cryptomeria*, cypresses, especially the bald or swamp cypress (*Taxodium distichum*), wild olives, *Celtis*, *Senegalia / Vachellia*, elms, *Zelkova* and maples. Deciduous trees are highly recommended for their spectacular autumn, winter and spring displays.

Chinese-originated styles

Penjin style

Horai style

Exposed root style – Ne-agari

Octopus style – Tako-zukuri

Plaited trunk style – Pien-tshu (Karame-miki)

This is a typical example of the mood of Penjin. The tree belongs to Mr Luu Truongson.

Penjin style

Penjin can be regarded as the oldest school in the cultivation of miniature trees. The second oldest school is the traditional Japanese school of bonsai which was founded during the tenth and eleventh centuries. The third is the African school of bonsai which includes the well-known Pierneef (or open umbrella canopy) and the baobab as prime examples.

Penjin has a long and fascinating history. Wall paintings of miniature trees were recorded as far back as 200 BC, and the art of bonsai, as we know it today, has been flourishing ever since. The art of cultivating miniature trees is called 'penzai' in Chinese, which is the equivalent name for bonsai.

These miniature trees were smuggled into Japan by Buddhist monks during the tenth and eleventh centuries. As far as we know, the monks were educated people, and they were regarded as literate men in China. The well-known literati style was the brainchild of these monks, and even today it is still regarded as the highest form in which the art of bonsai, or penzai, can be expressed.

The Penjin style is an expression of life and as such it is not bound by convention or rules. It is also closely intertwined with Chinese philosophy and culture. Penjin is therefore not a mere reproduction of nature – a tree or a landscape in the Penjin style is an attempt by the artist to create a work of art that expresses a particular atmosphere or mood.

Penjin is a broad term assigned to Chinese landscape paintings and horticultural artworks, which include single trees as well as miniature landscapes. Every Penjin design tells a story, because a great deal of symbolism is woven into each creation.

The Chinese choose enchanting, poetic names for their trees. Here are a few examples:

- An old lady makes herself beautiful
- Sculpture in green jade
- Green bells ringing in the morning
- The tiger slumbers
- An apple tree puts on its red dress
- The dragon flies into the sky.

This tree by Mr Luu Truongson perfectly captures the tone and feeling of the Penjin style.

Guidelines for creating the Penjin style

General points

A good Penjin need not always be dramatic and need not always have strong lines; it could also have a natural appearance. However, to emphasise the drama of Penjin, the foliage should be well clipped to form small clouds or discs.

- Negative space is of the utmost importance to the Chinese artist as it not only highlights the trunk lines, but also creates perspective and depth, which in turn enhance the dramatic effect of the style.
- Other important elements of Penjin are form, texture of the bark and jins, which are regarded as the scars of life.

Penjin styles

Penjin can be classified by shape and form as well as different techniques advocated by the various Penjin Schools.

For example, the 'cut and grow technique' of the Lingnan School is used all over the world by almost all bonsai growers. The technique can be summarised as follows:

- The tree is pruned back to its basic structure.
- New shoots are allowed to grow out until they reach the required size.
- The new shoots are then cut back again.

By using this technique the tree is shaped according to the correct proportions between trunk, main branches, side branches, twiggy growth, etc.

Penjin can also be classified according to the shape of the tree. There are six traditional shapes:

- the upright shape
- the crooked shape (the trunk curves upwards like a snake)
- reclining or lying down shape (reminiscent of the fallen tree shape or the raft style)
- overhanging cliff shape (similar to the cascade style)
- root shape (which is in fact the exposed root style)
- jungle shape (which includes all natural tree forms).

Well-known Penjin styles

The following are sketches of famous Chinese and local trees in the Penjin style.

A peaceful scene created by Mr Luu Truongson. Figurines often feature in Penjin creations.

For the Chinese, Penjin means the overall impact the tree has on its viewer as well as the emotions it arouses. The correct taper and position of the branches are therefore unimportant. Furthermore, a tired stranger will not count nor criticise the branches that give welcome shade from the sun.

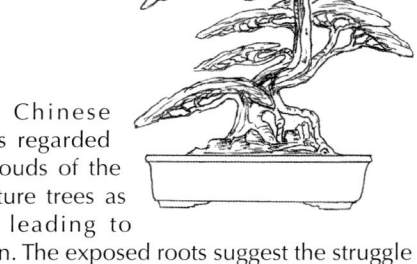

Early Chinese monks regarded the clouds of the miniature trees as steps leading to heaven. The exposed roots suggest the struggle for survival. The trunk line is of great importance to the Chinese: therefore it should be dramatic and full of character.

Planted in a deep pot and with its branches shaped in compact clouds, this tree has an aura of peace. The Chinese's love of nature is evident in this Penjin; although the design is dramatic, the tree still appears completely natural.

The lizard-shaped stone and the shari on the tree complement each other. The Chinese have a strong appreciation of form and texture. The tree in the sketch can be seen in the Wan Jing Shan Zhuang Garden in China.

This elm Penjin gives an impression of strength and stability. Bulky trunked Penjin are usually planted in deep pots to create the illusion of stability and strength. The original tree is 90 cm high and can be seen in the Zhuo Zheng Garden in China.

The exaggerated long trunk with its various platforms or clouds extends over the mountain, reaching for the sky. This Penjin evokes a feeling of peace and tranquillity. The foliage layers, which are kept compact, create depth and spaciousness.

As mentioned earlier, a Penjin is not judged by rules but rather by the mood it imparts. The slanting trunk with its delicate lines directs the eye towards the neatly formed crown. The Chinese do not believe in creating a perfect tree, but rather in setting a mood or conveying a philosophical theme which can be admired by all.

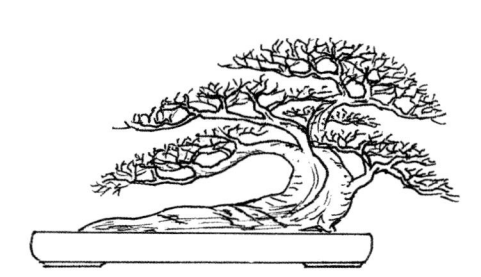

The reclining shape, which resembles the well-known raft style, is a recognised shape in Penjin. The difference between the two styles is found in the horizontal tree trunk, which is the dominant feature in this Penjin, whereas the tree trunk in the raft style is of lesser importance.

The gnarled old trunk reminds one of a beast resting in the shade of a tree. The tree overpowers the distant miniature stone monastery, which provides depth to the creation.

In this Penjin a sense of peacefulness is depicted by the figure sitting under a tree near a lake. Figurines or figure stones are often seen in Penjin creations.

'The praying mantis ready to pounce on its prey'! Originally, this tree was an uninteresting cascade but the owner transformed it into this dramatic Penjin. The dramatic impact of the tree is heightened by the way the branches are placed. Foliage is kept dense and to the minimum.

'Rearing horse in front of two pagodas'. The trunk of this ancient Penjin is almost completely dead. Only a narrow strip of bark keeps the top portion alive. This *Sageretia* tree is 40 cm high. According to the Chinese, a well-designed tree always tells a story. The story behind this creation is that the gallant prince is on his way to take the beautiful princess as his bride.

'The Night of Literati' – the sentimental mood pays homage to the moon shadow. This presentation of a poetic subject by Robert Steven was the runner-up at the Ben Oki International Design Awards in 2002. The tree is a *Pemphis acidula*. Height 35 cm.

This delicate twin-trunk *Celtis*, collected by the author in the veldt, has been trained into a drooping form. This tree is called 'Green bells ringing in the morning' and one can almost hear the crystal clear tinkling of the bells. The tree is 75 cm high.

Containers

Containers play a vital role in the creation of a Penjin work of art. The appropriate container not only accentuates line and form, but also adds to the aura surrounding the tree.

Deep bulky containers, normally used for semi-cascades, are also used for thick-trunked trees. In most cases, trees look over-potted, but the main aim should be to create an impression of stability and strength.

Shallow containers can be used for delicate trees. The containers in the sketches are typical of the ones used for Penjin creations.

Horai style

Horai is another style that originated in China. As with most Chinese styles, these creations tell a story or express a particular mood. The strangely curved and twisted trunks and branches, typical of the Horai style, are symbolic of dragons, hermits and hunchbacks wandering in the woods. Despite their struggle for survival against the elements, these trees emanate a sense of dignity.

The contorted and twisted trunks of the Horai style evoke images of mythical creatures like dragons and snakes. The trees on this page have been styled by Mr Luu Truongson.

Guidelines for creating the Horai style

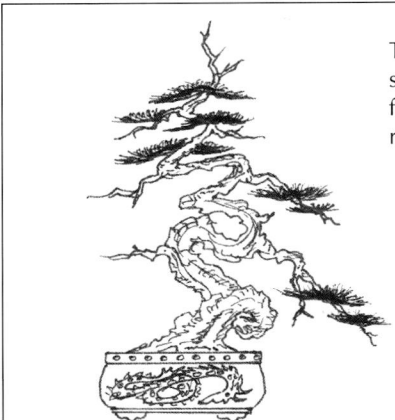

The typically twisted trunk with jins suggests a dragon with its spines raised and claws reaching out through the clouds. The foliage is sparse to emphasise the movement of the dragon. A richly engraved pot completes the scene.

'The python strikes again' – the aggression of the snake is depicted in this tree. To succeed in creating a three-dimensional effect, the bends should not only vary in size but also curve backwards, upwards and downwards. Back branches are important to create depth and perspective in a style. A deep drum-shaped container adds to the rugged appearance of the tree.

Not all Horai-styled trees allude to dragons or pythons. The main aim of the Horai style is to emphasise the exaggerated curves in the trunk and branch lines. The curves and overlip of the container emphasise the movement of the trunk and the tapered legs help to give an airy feeling to the composition.

Containers

Chinese pots, intricately engraved with dragons or Chinese poems (which almost always relate to nature), are well suited to the Horai style. Drum-shaped containers also add to the atmosphere of the orient. As most trees are twisted and curved, oval or round containers help to accentuate the movement of the trees.

Plant material

Pines and conifers are normally used in Horai styles. Deciduous trees with small leaves can also be used.

176

Exposed root style – Ne-agari

Although not often seen in bonsai collections, the exposed root style is one of the most interesting and also one of the most artistic styles in Pensai. The exaggerated long roots bring to mind the age of the dinosaurs.

The style is divided into two main categories:
- an artistic and exaggerated Ne-agari style where the roots are at least half to two-thirds the length of the tree
- a more natural style where the roots are similar to those seen in nature.

This five-needle pine (*Pinus pentaphylla* var. *himekomatsu*) is an outstanding example of a true exposed root style. The tree was originally collected from the Azuma Mountains. The exposure of the roots is artistically executed and the tree has an feeling of harmony and movement. Part of the late Mr Iwasaki's collection.

Guidelines for creating the exposed root style

Artistic or exaggerated styles

Informal Ne-agari

As in most of the Chinese-style trees, the emphasis is on dramatic effects. The foliage is sparse and in balance with the root framework. A hexagonal pot lends a delicate but stable feeling to the composition.

Slanting Ne-agari

The trunk leans over to give a slanting effect. Although it might look unnatural, these forms do exist in nature. The tree not only has a pleasing appearance, but also gives an impression of strength and endurance. The style requires skill to avoid a puny, leggy appearance that lacks charm. A round dish-like pot rounds off the composition.

Cascading Ne-agari

The roots form the main focal point and should be at least two-thirds of the length of the tree. The round literati-shaped container gives stability to the creation.

Waterfall Ne-agari

The tree simulates a waterfall cascading down a cliff, which is formed by the exposed roots. In nature, erosion is often the cause of exposed roots, especially along riverbeds or waterfalls. A dish-like container complements the scene.

Windswept Ne-agari

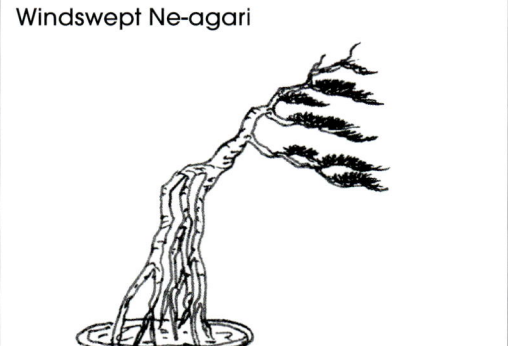

This pared-down design echoes the literati style, where less is more.

Typical aerial roots of the *Ficus thonningii*, grown and styled by Dr Tobie Kleynhans.

Exposed-root styles found in nature

Buttressed root style

The buttressed roots of some *Ficus* species create an interesting variation of the Ne-agari style. The roots normally grow flat and upright, like walls around the trunk. This phenomenon is found only on very old fig trees. An oval container or slate works well to accommodate the magnificent roots.

Aerial root style

Aerial roots fit in with the exposed-roots phenomenon. These roots are common among the *Ficus* species and give another dimension to the Ne-agari style. The strangling fig (*Ficus thonningii*) is a fine example of this style.

Exposed roots due to erosion

One often finds that the roots of trees growing next to the water's edge become exposed because the soil has been washed away by floods. A deep oval container harmonises with the mass foliage of this style.

Plaited or twisted root style

The plaited root style should look strangled but natural. Avoid artificial plaited roots that look like the plait on the head of a teenage girl. A rectangular container gives stability to the unstable mood reflected by the roots.

Containers

As shown in the sketches, literati pots, i.e. round, dish-like or hexagonal, emphasise the artistic and exaggerated exposed root styles. The more natural Ne-agari styles may be planted in oval or rectangular containers or on slate.

Plant material

Any plant material can be used for the style. Pines, conifers and *Ficus* species, however, are best suited to the exaggerated styles.

Octopus style – Tako-zukuri

Although this style is seldom seen in bonsai collections, it is another Chinese style with an elaborate appearance. Most of the tree's character emanates from the long curving branches which reach out like the tentacles of an octopus.

This Sargent's juniper is a fine example of the octopus style. It is found in the National Arboretum in Washington.

Guidelines for creating the octopus style

Clump octopus style

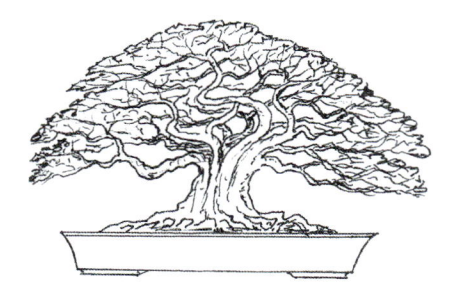

Trees like these, with their branches intermingled and stretching out in search of sunlight, are often seen in coastal areas. The widespread gnarled roots add to the character of the tree. The oval container accentuates the movement of the branches.

Slanted octopus style

The long branches with their curves and loops are reminiscent of the tentacles of an octopus. Trees growing in this fashion are often seen in nature. A deep oval container complements the creation.

Extreme octopus style

The tree in the sketch brings to mind ancient tales of dragons and other fabulous creatures – in this case an octopus stretching out its tentacles in search of prey. Although over-exaggerated, the tree still has beauty and charm. A drum-shaped container complements the tree.

Containers

Oval and round containers are normally used as they capture the branch and trunk movements which are the key feature of the octopus style.

Plant material

Any plant material, such as conifers and small-leafed trees, may be used for the style.

This tree suggests an octopus catching its prey. The tree belongs to Mr Luu Truongson from China.

181

Plaited trunk style – Pien-tshu (Karame-miki)

The plaited style is also Chinese in origin. In this style the entwined vines form the trunk. This can be an intriguing style, especially when young material is used. After some years, the vines will fuse together to form a distinctive twisted old trunk.

This wild apricot (*Dovyalis zeyheri*), designed by the author, consists of two separate trees intertwined together.

Guidelines for creating the plaited trunk style

Five or more young pliable plants, e.g. certain *Ficus* species, can be plaited together. The ends of the individual trunks form the main branches. Just make sure that the entwined trunk does not look like a plait of hair.

Vines are the ideal plant material for this twined and tangled plaited tree. The trunks will fuse as the plants grow older to give an interesting and gnarled appearance. An oval container adds to the movement of the style.

How the plaited tree style should not look. A tree plaited like a string of hair not only looks unnatural but is an injustice to the style.

Containers

Oval or round containers are most suitable for the style as they emphasise the movement of the tree.

Plant material

Vines such as *Wisteria*, *Bougainvillaea* and honeysuckle (*Lonicera*), groundcovers such as ivy (*Hedera*) as well as some conifers are suited to the style. Indigenous plant species such as Pride of the Cape (*Bauhinea galpinii*) and Cape honeysuckle (*Tecomaria capensis*) can also be used. *Ficus* species are an excellent choice as they are pliable and fuse easily when the plant gets older.

African styles

The styles in this section were created by the author as the 'Third School of Bonsai', namely the African School of Bonsai.

Baobab style

Pierneef style

Flat Top style

Bushveld or natural style – 'Shizen-zukuri'

Wild fig style

Elbow or 'Wonderboom' style

A young baobab tree owned and styled by Hennie Smit.

Baobab style

The baobab is a native tree which grows in the drier tropical parts of Africa. It is found from the Tropic of Capricorn to as far north as Egypt. Furthermore, it has been described more frequently than any other tree in Africa, e.g. an account of the tree appeared in a historical publication in Egypt as far back as 1592.

Of all the trees in the world there is none more grotesque. This enormous, and sometimes odd-shaped, tree fascinates all who see it. Some botanists depict the baobab as a monarch, a monster of a prehistorical world, a vegetable elephant, or a carrot growing upside-down, while some African tribes call it 'the tree that has been planted upside-down by the gods'.

This tree is not known for its height, which could be in the region of fourteen to twenty metres, but for its enormous girth. Livingstone, the great explorer (1813–1873), apparently once camped under a baobab with a circumference of twenty-six metres.

Baobab trees are remarkably tough. They can withstand the worst droughts and, if their bark gets damaged by humans or elephants, they will simply grow another bark and continue to flourish. Livingstone wrote in one of his diaries that 'No external injury, not even a fire, can destroy this tree from without; nor can any injury be done from within, as it is quite common to find it hollow ….. Nor does cutting down exterminate it, for I saw instances in Angola in which it continued to grow in length after it was lying on the ground'.

African tribes believe the baobab is immortal. It is therefore preserved as a holy tree. Many tribal chiefs are buried in the shade of these huge trees. A baobab can live for thousands of years: The oldest recorded baobab is more than three thousand years old.

Many a spectator is left breathless when he or she sees a baobab for the first time. No wonder that one of the great bonsai masters, John Naka, after his first visit to Africa, wrote in a letter: 'I am especially happy to see you utilising your own native materials, such as acacia, wild olive, etc. … but most of all, that great super baobab tree. I was so overwhelmed by that tree and the greatness of nature, I felt like a tiny piece of dust lying on the mountain. I feel that the baobab tree can become a bonsai model for your part of the country'.

The baobab style is indeed unique, and one of the styles created by the author.

An older version of a baobab tree owned by Johan Ras.

Guidelines for creating the baobab style

Formal upright style

Interrupted trunk line

The traditional baobab style has the following features:
- an interrupted trunk line which should radiate a masculine mood
- a straight trunk.

The trunk forms the focal point and should therefore impart a feeling of strength and stability. It should be free of side branches, and its length could vary between one-third to half the size of the tree.

The sketch shows a young baobab with an upright branch structure. The impressive trunk, which is perfectly straight and does not taper towards the apex, is the main point of interest. The main branches emerge from the same spot on the trunk and stretch out into the sky like monstrous arms. The branch formation is similar to that of the broom style, except that it is informal and grotesque.

The height of the trunk can vary. The large circumference of the short trunk signifies a tree of great age.

Continuous trunk line

The uninterrupted trunk line from the root base to the apex appears in nature, although it is seldom seen. The heavy branches are still the trademark of the style, but the silhouette line tends to favour the flame shape.

Variations on the baobab style

Informal upright style

In the informal upright style the trunk line is slightly curved. In nature the baobab does not have a definite main-root system, but in bonsai a few main roots may be displayed. A deep container with an overlip is used to emphasise the huge trunk.

Slanting style

Although the trunk slants to the left, no major branch alterations are necessary to create this style. The main branch on the right, however, tends to develop more rapidly than the one on the left. The round crown remains a dominant feature.

An oval-shaped crown with a dominant side branch

The prominent branch on the left complements the continuous trunk line. The deep oval container echoes the movement of the oval-shaped crown.

Double trunk style (Sokan)

The two trunks share the same root system. The upper silhouette line has the shape of an open umbrella. The twin-trunk style (Soju) can also be created by simply planting two trees closely together.

Turtle-back or stump style (Korabuki)

The swollen base, representing a tortoise-shell, together with the multiple trunks sprouting from the main trunk, makes it a very interesting style.

A corkwood tree (*Commiphora harveyi*) grown by Derick Veldhuizen in the baobab style.

Clump or sprout style (Kabudachi)

Seven main trunks form this interesting clump style. The trunks develop from the same root system and bend sideways in search of sunlight. A deep rectangular container emphasises the massive trunk.

A Saikei group of three trees

The trees are planted on slate and the landscape is rounded off with weathered stones and red sand, which simulate the severe conditions in which the baobabs are usually found. The trunk movement of the two main trees has been impeded by placing the younger one close to the main tree.

Livingstone's tree

A tree similar to the one in the sketch was recorded by Livingstone south of Gootsa Pan in Botswana in the late 1800s, and can still be seen at the site. The tree in the sketch is a fine example of the baobab style: in nature a tree of this size can have a circumference of up to twenty-six metres. This tree is believed to be more than 3 000 years old.

Group planting (Yose-uye)

Two dominant trees form the focal point. As the baobab is grotesque in appearance, the group should consist of not more than five to seven trees, depending on the size of the container. A deep oval container will be the best choice for this style.

Literati baobab style

This is a style one could also attempt, even though it is seldom seen in nature. Only young baobab trees should be used, as they tend to be lanky in appearance. Further-more, a continuous trunk line is vital for creating a literati ef-fect. A replica of the tree in the sketch is growing near the Vic-toria Falls in Zimbabwe.

Octopus baobab style

The wraith-like boughs resemble an octopus poised to seize its prey. An old-world charm radiates from this Chinese version of the octo-pus style. The original tree can be found near Thabazimbi in the Limpopo Province. This odd-shaped tree also symbol-ises a carrot monster, or a vegetable el-ephant, or any other image that captures the mind.

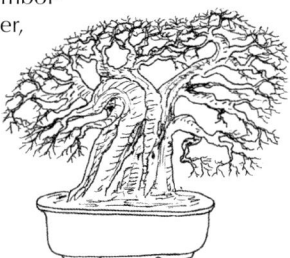

Hollow trunk style

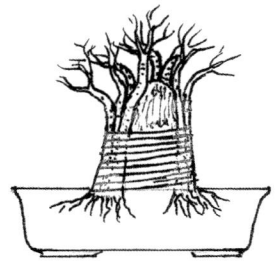

It is not uncommon to find a baobab with a hollow trunk, and old baobabs quite often have a hollow trunk. African tribes sometimes deliberately hollow out the spongy wood to create a storage space or a human shelter.

Creating a baobab style with young plant material

Young trees, especially *Ficus* or *Erythrina* species, can be planted side by side against a round weathered log or a piece of polystyrene, and the trees tied together with raffia. The trees will eventually fuse and form branches which can be trained into the open umbrella shape.

Containers

Deep oval, round or rectangular containers are suitable. However, to emphasise the movement of the round crowns, oval containers are the best choice. If you wish to emphasise the large trunk and add stability to the style, use a pot with an overlip.

Plant material

Apart from the baobab (*Adansonia digitata*), other softwood species such as the coral tree (*Erythrina* species), corkwood (*Commiphora* species) or the belambra tree (*Phytolacca dioica*) can be trained into the baobab style with great success. Evergreens or deciduous trees with thick trunks may also be used.

Pierneef style

The Pierneef style, or open umbrella shape, is unique to Africa. The continent boasts an incredibly rich floral diversity but the thorn trees (previously known as the genus *Acacia* but now classified under *Senegalia* and *Vachellia*) are an iconic feature of the African landscape. Thorn trees are closely associated with the African veldt where buffalo, wildebeest, zebra, giraffe and lion roam.

These superb trees with their semi-circular crowns, like open umbrellas, inspired the author to develop a new African style. The umbrella-shaped form was spontaneously named after the well-known Pretoria artist Jacob Hendrik Pierneef who depicted many of these tree forms in his paintings (see box on next page).

One could sum up the Pierneef concept in a nutshell as follows: all the rules of bonsai still apply and form the basis of the approach, except that the triangular concept has been replaced by semi-circles or open umbrellas.

The Pierneef concept is therefore not restricted to a single style but includes styles such as the informal, slanting, twin trunk, three and five trunk, multiple trunk, group planting, hollow trunk, split trunk, root-over-rock and the literati style or free style.

Styles which definitely do not suit the Pierneef approach are the formal upright, full cascade, windswept and willow styles as well as some of the minor styles.

It is therefore clear that the Pierneef approach is a broad and overarching concept. Although the Pierneef concept has been developed with the African thorn trees (*Senegalia* and *Vachellia* species; previously *Acacia*) in mind, other plant materials may also be used.

This raintree was originally styled by the author into the Pierneef style in 2005 at the Fifth World Bonsai Convention in Washington [inset]. The basic framework was bought by Erik Wigert of Wigert's Bonsai Nursery in Florida. Erik developed the tree into this outstanding Pierneef style.

Thorn trees depicted in Pierneef's art

Pierneef's affinity for thorn trees in their natural habitat is evident from the following linocut and sketches among many of his other works.

Thorn Tree and House: This linocut could be classified as a literati style because of its elegant form and trunk line.

Thorn Tree and Landscape: The tree in this sketch served as the inspiration for the logo of the Pretoria Bonsai-Kai, and is regarded as an ideal informal Pierneef style.

Thorn Trees Rustenburg: Another of Pierneef's outstanding sketches. Note the interesting branch structure and especially the main tree, which can be classified as the double trunk style.

Guidelines for creating the Pierneef style

Roots

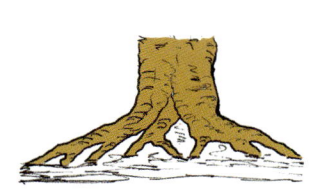

As in most styles, the roots form the basis of the trunk and they should therefore be evenly spread round the trunk.

Trunk

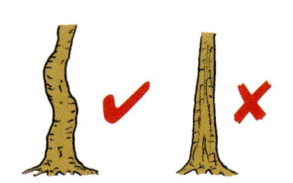

The trunk is always informal and therefore curved. A formal upright trunk is not suitable because the Pierneef style is an informal and natural style.

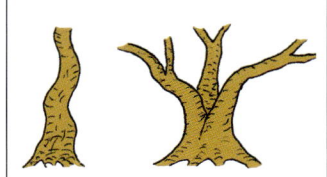

The trunk may be single or multiple.

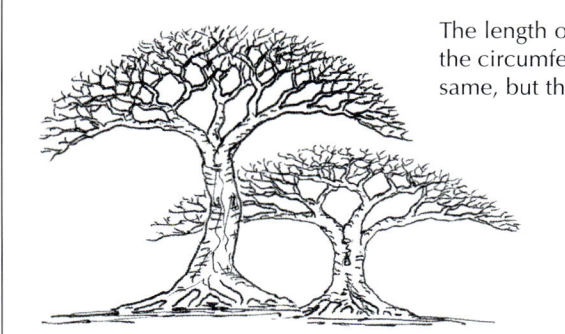

The length of the trunk may vary in height. For instance the circumference of the two crowns in the sketch is the same, but the two trunks differ in length.

Crowns

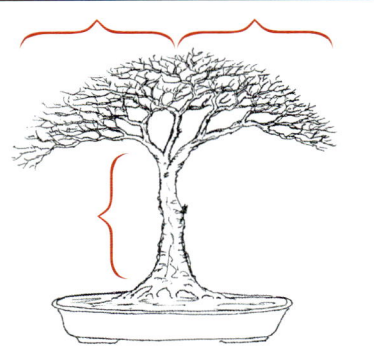

The circumference of the crown should be twice the length of the trunk. However, this rule does not apply to shorter trunks which can have a crown-to-trunk ratio of six to one.

The Pierneef style is not restricted to one crown and can have two or more crowns according to the branch structure.

Branch structure

Main branches

The trunk normally forks into two, three or five main branches. The three-branch structure is considered to be the best option.

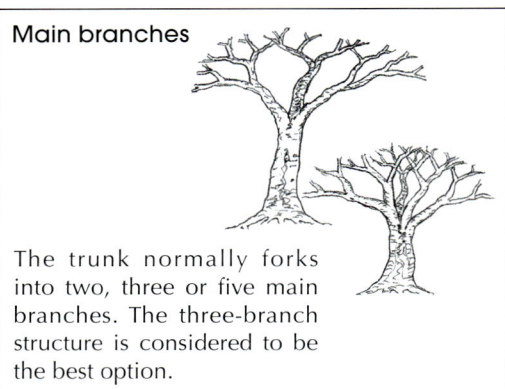

Branch structure as seen from above

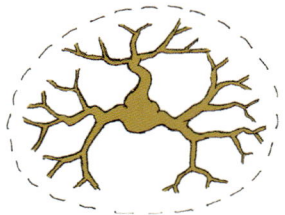

Two of the main branches developed to the sides and slightly to the front. The other branch is placed to the back to create depth.

Branch subdivision

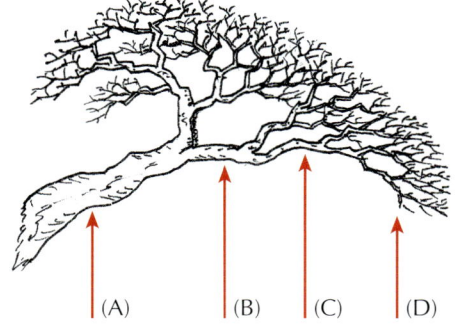

(A)   (B)   (C)   (D)

The main branch (A) divides into secondary branches (B), which in turn subdivide into tertiary branches (C) and eventually form the twiggy growth (D) on which the leaves grow.

Basic branch structure of the Pierneef style

The sketch shows a schematic construction of the branch structure. The branches continually divide into smaller forks which eventually form the twiggy growth. The tree bears its leaves only on the twiggy growth, which then results in the traditional Pierneef umbrella.

The crown of the Pierneef forms a semi-circle and that of the broom a full circle. The continuous zigzag pattern is the trademark of the informal branch structure of the Pierneef style. Note that the container is deeper than the one used for the broom style.

The difference between the broom and the Pierneef styles lies in the branch structure. The Pierneef has an informal zigzag structure whereas the broom has a formal and more graceful structure.

Variations on the Pierneef style

Informal Pierneef style

The Pierneef style symbolises an informal tree with lots of movement. The trunk is curved, and the structure of the main and secondary branches is well developed to support the tertiary and fine growth of the tree. The crown forms an open umbrella, which is the trademark of the style.

Slanting Pierneef style

The tree has an elegant appearance. The crown covers most of the space in the container. It is planted to one side of the container with the trunk leaning towards the opposite side. The oval container complements the movement of the crown.

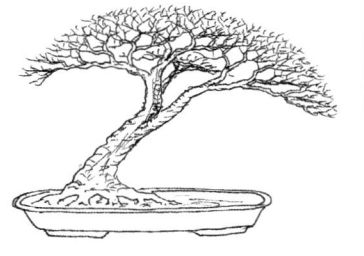

Low-forked Pierneef style

These low-forked trees are a typical phenomenon found in nature and have an appealing effect on the viewer. An oval container echoes the crown's movement.

Double-trunk Pierneef or Sokan style

In the Sokan style the trees share the same root system. A single crown usually suits this style the best. An oval container rounds off the composition.

193

Twin-trunk Pierneef or Soju style

The two trees form a harmonious composition. The size of the two trees can vary considerably, as long as the trees radiate a feeling of harmony and unity. The length of the container should be slightly less than the width of the crowns.

Triple-trunk Pierneef or Sankan style

The main tree is planted in the centre and the two minor trees towards the sides, to create depth. The main tree could also be planted on the outside of the arrangement to create a different mood. The oval container complements the movement of the crowns.

Clump or sprout Pierneef style

To create the clump style, you need five or seven trunks growing from the same root base. Closely planted trunks will also serve the purpose, as will either a single crown or multiple crowns. The depth of the container should equal the width of the trunk.

Split trunk Pierneef style

The split in the trunk may have been caused by either strong winds or lightning. The major trunk gives balance to the creation and it should therefore be the biggest. The tree may have a single crown or two separate crowns. The oval container complements the scene.

Hollow trunk Pierneef style

The hollow trunk, which may have been caused by termites, adds to the character of the tree. Only very large trunks should be used for this creation. The crown could be single or multiple. The deep oval container matches the trunk's width.

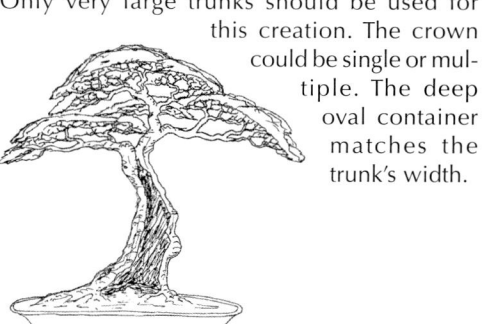

Root-over-rock Pierneef style

Thorn trees are normally found in savanna and open bushveld, therefore the rock should conjure up a picture of a distant mountain or a rocky outcrop. Do not place the tree on top of the rock but rather towards the side, to accentuate the landscape. The long oval container helps to draw attention to the landscape.

Pierneef group styles

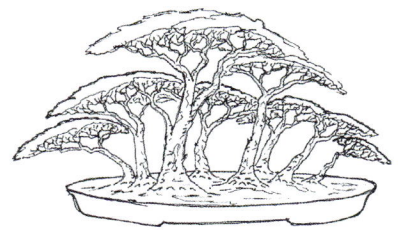

Close-view group design: The two main trees are planted towards the front to suggest a near or close view; smaller trees are planted at the sides and back to give the necessary depth.

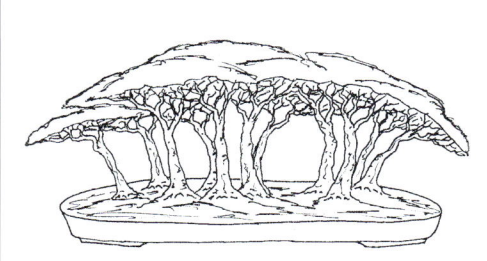

Distant-view group design: In the distant view, the emphasis is on the silhouette line which forms a single crown. Use trees of the same size to highlight this effect. A flat oval container complements the creation.

Bushveld group: The main tree is the focal point of this Saikei. The scene portrays a group of thorn trees in their natural habitat and includes a rocky outcrop or even anthills so typical of the open bushveld.

Literati Pierneef style

In his book *Bonsai Techniques II,* John Naka drew this tree in the literati style Pierneef from a photograph taken of a young African thorn tree growing in the Kruger National Park. The diversity of the Pierneef concept is well showcased in this literati creation. Note the delicate branch structure.

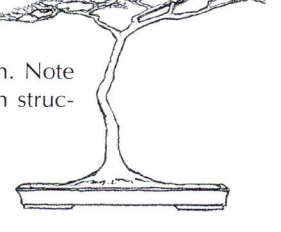

A typical Pierneef-style *Buddleja saligna,* styled by the late Mr Louis Nel.

Containers

To complement the round umbrella crowns of the style, it is best to use oval or round containers. Like most indigenous trees in this country, the thorn trees (*Senegalia / Vachellia* species) prefer deep containers. To allow for the needs of the tree, it is permissible to somewhat overpot. As a point of interest, azaleas also grow better in deep containers.

Plant material

Although it is obvious that the various *Senegalia / Vachellia* species are the best choice for the Pierneef style, you may also use other plant material such as the elm, maple, *Celtis, Olea,* and many other species to interpret this style.

Flat Top style

The flat top style has its origin in two African thorn trees: the paperbark thorn (*Vachellia sieberiana* var. *woodii*) and the Nyanga flat top (*Vachellia abyssinica*). These magnificent trees are found in the warmer parts of Africa and have a particular branch formation which inspired the author to create a unique African style.

The paperbark thorn, also called the flat top acacia, is usually found in grassland and bushveld in the eastern lowveld and northern parts of KwaZulu-Natal. It is a huge deciduous tree with wide-spreading branches which form a flattened circle similar to the spokes of a wheel when viewed from above.

The Inyanga flat, found in Ethiopia, is more distinctively flat-topped, has a more slender trunk and a more delicate overall appearance compared to the paperbark thorn.

An interesting characteristic of these two trees is that the top growth is short, hence the unique flat top.

HAIKU
Flat top Acacia,
rugged trunk.
Siesta to strangers
passing by

This thorn tree (*Senegalia burkei*) is an excellent example of the flat top style. The tree belongs to Org Exley.

Guidelines for creating the flat top style

Branch structure

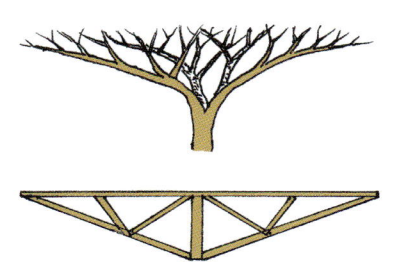

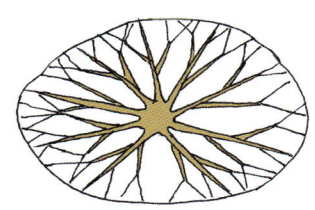

The branch structure of the flat top style resembles a funnel or an inverted roof truss exposing the beams and rafters. The main branches stretch out towards the outer circle of the framework and form the basis of the style.

Looking at the design from above, the main branches are spread out to form a flattened circle, which resembles the spokes of a wheel. The front and back branches are shorter than those at the outer sides and form an ellipse. The side branches are placed alternately on the sides of the main branches.

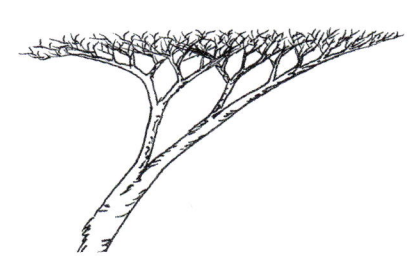

The sketch shows a typical branch structure of the flat top style. The secondary branches grow all along the main branch and form a slanting flat crown in their search for sunlight.

Branch length

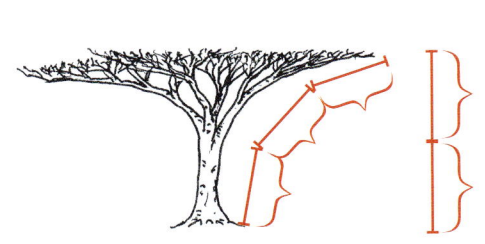

The length of a main branch plus the length of the trunk should be one-third longer than the height of the tree. Should the main branches be shorter, the style would lose its unique character and the tree would revert to a Pierneef style without the typical umbrella crown.

Roots and trunk line

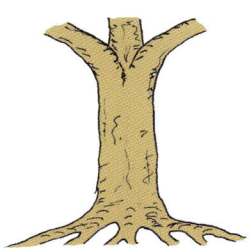

The roots should spread evenly round the trunk and should be without deformities, i.e. no octopus or curled roots which would ruin the elegant beauty of the style. The trunk should be fairly straight to the point where the main branches fork out. It may curve slightly but not too acutely. The flat top style usually has an interrupted trunk line.

Branch line

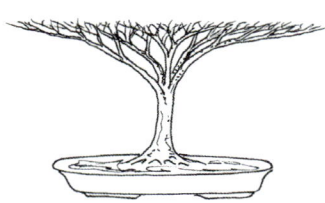

The basic structure of the style usually consists of three, five or seven main branches, which curve softly towards the tips and spread around the trunk to form a circle or an ellipse.

An *asymmetrical branch placement* is recommended as it gives greater movement and rhythm to the style. The crowns may be layered like slices on top of each other. Similar to the broom style, the flat top style has a fairly formal appearance.

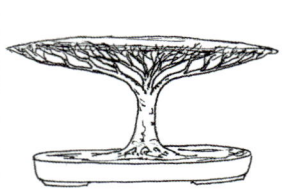

A *symmetrical branch placement* is possible but could lack rhythm and appear stilted.

Silhouette line

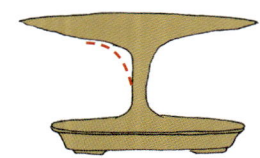

The sketch shows the silhouette line of a symmetrical branch placement. The dotted line indicates the silhouette line of an asymmetrical branch placement.

Variations on the flat top style

Single trunk flat top

The main branch structure usually starts halfway up the trunk. There is a flattened zigzag pattern similar to the Pierneef style and the branches extend sideways to form the flat top. An oval container captures the movement of the flat crown.

Double-trunk flat top

The trunk splits into two or three main branches quite close to its base. Side branches tend to be slightly longer, and also more elegant, than those of the flattened structure of a single-trunk tree.

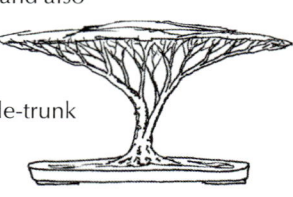

Short trunk flat top

The side branches of the short trunk flat top are inclined to extend much further than those in the preceding styles, resulting in a very wide crown. A deep oval container balances the visual weight of the crown.

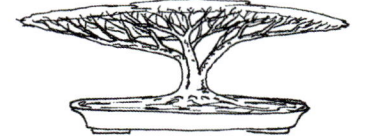

Clump style flat top

Five or more trunks are needed for the clump style. The trunks stretch out sideways in search of sunlight and so form an oval or a circle. To support the wide crown, the secondary branches are also longer than usual. A deep oval container complements the scene.

Flat top Sokan or triple-trunk arrangement	Flat top group arrangement
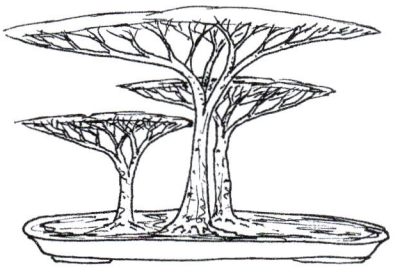	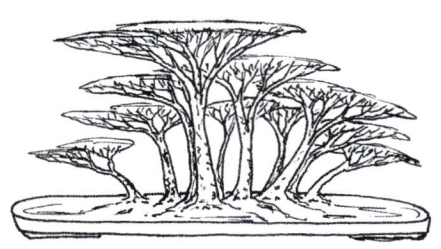
To create depth, the main tree is planted in the centre and the two minor trees towards the back. For a different scene or mood, the main tree could be planted on the outside of the grouping. A shallow oval container suggests a feeling of space and vastness.	To create a near-view group, the dominant tree is planted just off-centre and the supporting tree is planted behind it. A second main tree is planted next to the first one on the right-hand side, and smaller and supporting trees are grouped around the two main trees. A shallow long container heightens the effect of the group arrangement. The length of the container should be equal to the width of the crowns.

Containers

As shown in the sketches, oval containers are by far the most suitable as they echo the movement and rhythm of the curved branches and blend in with the flattish circular crowns.

Plant material

African thorn trees, especially *Vachellia* species, are the best choice for the style. However, other small-leafed plants, as well as some conifer species, may also be used. Broad-leaved plants are not suitable as the leaves would hide the prominent branch structure, which is the main focal point of the style.

This young tamarind tree (*Tamarindus indica*) has been styled into the flat top style by Mr Aslam Sulaiman of Pakistan.

Bushveld or natural style – Shizen-zukuri

In Afrikaans, the word 'bushveld' literally means 'land covered by trees'. The bushveld is a broad area found in the warmer subtropical parts of southern Africa, roughly between nine and twenty-six degrees latitude. Southern Africa is rich in plant life and hundreds of indigenous tree species are found in the bushveld habitat. Despite being a fairly dry area, the flora adapts exceptionally well to the arid climate.

Well-known bushveld tree species include the baobab, thorn trees (*Senegalia* and *Vachellia* species; previously *Acacia*), some *Ficus* species, marula (*Sclerocarya birrea*), mopane (*Colophospermum mopane*), tamboti (*Spirostachys africana*), leadwood or hardekool (*Combretum imberbe*), mountain syringa (*Kirkia wilmsii*) and many others. These trees have a natural growing habit and, as is the case with most tree species found in Africa, the branch structure is informal and zigzagged. The dry conditions shape the development of these trees, resulting in some unique tree forms.

The 'bushveld' or 'natural style' is therefore an appropriate description of the landscape. It is characterised by open savanna covered with trees, bringing to mind images of herds of antelope roaming the African plains with their predators in tow.

The style differs from the Pierneef, wild fig and informal broom styles in that it does not have a specific shape or form. For instance, the silhouette line may be oval, round or umbrella-shaped; the trunks and main branches may curve or even cross each other and the branches may also intertwine.

The main objective of the style is to create a natural scene that radiates an air of strength and endurance. As the style simulates hardship and struggle, the foliage should be sparse.

This *Acacia arabica* designed by Robert Steven radiates an air of strength and endurance.

Guidelines for creating the bushveld style

Trunk-line

Continuous trunk line

The trunk line continues to the apex and, because the aim is to achieve a natural appearance, it curves slightly. Main branches may intertwine or cross the trunk. An important point to remember is that the branches must point upwards.

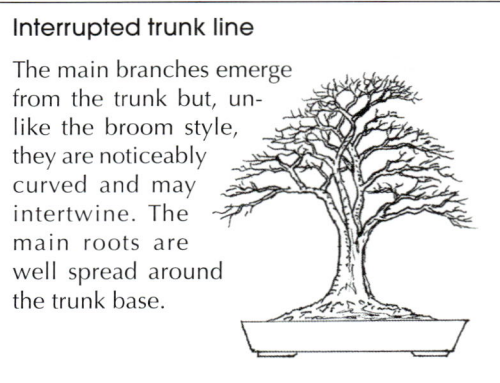

Interrupted trunk line

The main branches emerge from the trunk but, unlike the broom style, they are noticeably curved and may intertwine. The main roots are well spread around the trunk base.

Variations on the bushveld style

Double-trunk style (Sokan)

The trunk-lines are informal; the main branches grow upwards, and the smaller trunk leans away to accentuate the movement in the tree. The oval container harmonises with the crown's movement.

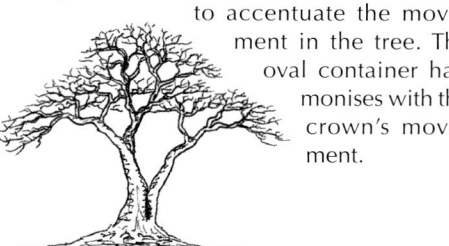

Slanting bushveld style

The slant towards the right alludes to a tree growing on a riverbank with its lowest branch spreading out over the water. The tree is planted slightly to the side of the container to emphasise the negative area, suggesting the edge of the stream.

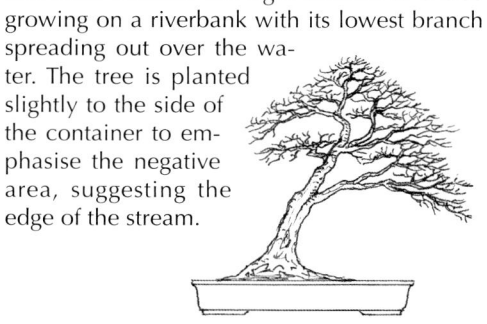

Gnarled trunk

This old tree slanting slightly to the left imparts a sense of great age and suffering while the curved branches are reminiscent of the octopus style. The deep rectangular container gives stability to the creation.

Short trunk bushveld style

The short trunk and low spreading branches depict another typical bushveld scene. The branches divide into sharp curves, which add to the beauty of the tree.

Clump style

Various trunks emerge from the same base to form this interesting clump style. The intertwining main branches are an acceptable feature of this style. The deep rectangular container complements the thick trunk and enhances the feeling of stability.

Bushveld group planting

The main trees in the centre of the group arrangement form the focal point. To create a group setting, you can use mixed species or trees of the same species. A shallow oval container or a flat stone is an excellent choice for this creation.

Containers

For trees that have round crowns, oval and round containers are recommended to capture the movement of the crowns. When the trunks are thick and rugged, deep rectangular containers add to the solid and stable appearance of the trees.

Plant material

Any plant material is suitable as long as a natural and informal appearance can be achieved. Avoid plants with lush green foliage as the bushveld style should give an impression of a harsh environment where plants struggle for survival against the elements.

This slanting Kei-apple (*Dovyalis caffra*) is a typical example of the bushveld style. This tree was started in 1973 from nursery stock by the author.

Wild fig style

The wild fig style can be regarded as a variation on the broom style. The dominant feature of the style is a full umbrella silhouette with an extremely wide branch span.

The widespread growing habit of these trees is characteristic of most *Ficus* species growing in the tropical parts of the world.

This Chinese banyan tree (*Ficus microcarpa*), grown by Dr Tobie Kleynhans, is a fine example of the wild fig style.

Guidelines for creating the wild fig style

Root system

Figs usually have a very widespread root system which extends in all directions around the trunk. Main roots are therefore encouraged to spread out further than usual.

Trunk

The trunk must be short with the length not exceeding one-third of the total height of the tree. The trunk line must be interrupted.

Branch construction

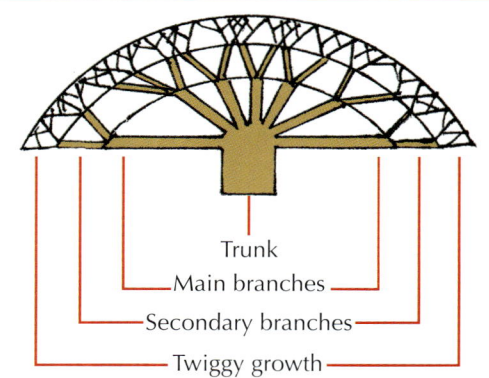

Trunk
Main branches
Secondary branches
Twiggy growth

The horizontal main branches are the longest, but they become shorter towards the centre. The structure consists of the trunk, main branches, secondary and tertiary branches and twiggy growth.

Subdivision of a main branch

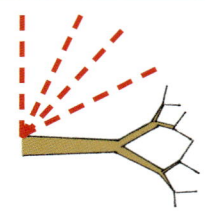

The main branch divides into two secondary branches, which in turn divide into tertiary branches to form the fine twiggy growth.

Silhouette line

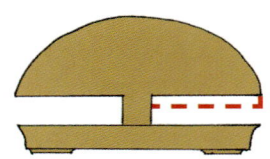

The silhouette line may be symmetrical or asymmetrical. The short thick trunk has a mushroom shape.

Variations on the wild fig style

Multiple-trunk style

The sketch depicts a multiple-trunk tree with a well-spread root system. This style symbolises not only strength and stability, but also peace and tranquillity. An oval container the same width as the crown is the most suitable choice.

Root-over-rock style

The root-over-rock style complements the huge crown. The lower branches stretch far out over the rock to add to the style's peaceful mood. The smaller twiggy growth tends to droop slightly.

Double trunk (Sokan)

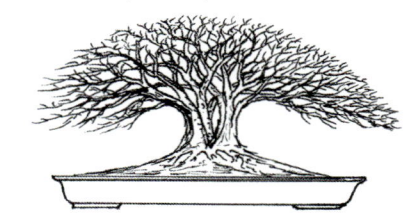

The round crown forms a neat canopy for the two trunks. The lower branches may be either symmetrical or asymmetrical.

Containers

Oval or round containers will complement the massive crown of the wild fig style. Because the crown is so compact, the container could be slightly deeper than normal. The length of the container should be the same as the crown's width. Evergreen trees may be planted in dark-brown terracotta pots, while deciduous trees show off better in light-coloured pots.

Plant material

Any evergreen or deciduous plant material is suitable for the style. However, *Ficus* species are regarded as the most suitable because they grow naturally into this particular style.

Elbow or 'Wonderboom' style

The elbow or 'Wonderboom' style is another uniquely African style created by the author. It was inspired by an extraordinary huge and famous wild fig tree, known as the 'Wonderboom', growing on the northern foothills of the Magalies mountain range on the outskirts of the city of Pretoria. The species was originally named *Ficus pretoriae*, after the city of Pretoria, but was later renamed *Ficus cordata* subsp. *salicifolia*. Its common name is the wonderboom fig – 'wonderboom' means 'wonder tree' or 'unique tree'.

Like the baobab, the Wonderboom tree in Pretoria is a true wonder of nature and a huge tourist attraction. This particular tree, or rather group of trees, has its origin in a natural layering process: Over the centuries the long spreading branches started to grow downwards and came to rest on the ground like an old man resting on his elbows. The huge branches then took root and sent up new trees. Several of these branches, in turn, gave rise to a third circle of trees. But some of the original branches have since decayed.

Today the 'Wonderboom' has a spread of fifty-five metres and a height of approximately twenty-five metres. One thousand one hundred people can sit in the shade of this unique tree. It is believed that the tree has been allowed to grow unmolested because the area around it is held sacred by the Ndebele tribe, as one of their chiefs was buried nearby the tree. They also believe that the tree attained its present colossal size owing to this fact.

The Wonderboom grove of mother and daughter trees at the Wonderboom Nature Reserve in Pretoria.

Guidelines for creating the elbow style

Natural layering method of the elbow style

The main branches of the Wonderboom fig became too heavy to continue growing upright and eventually came to rest on the ground where they started to take root. A new tree developed but it remained attached to the mother plant by way of the existing main branches.

Propagation system

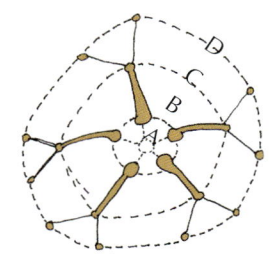

The Wonderboom fig in Pretoria started off as a single tree (A) one thousand years ago. The first set of elbows (B) were formed, then the second (C), and over the years the same process repeated itself to form the next set (D). Because of this process, the tree's crown increased resulting in its present huge crown. The original trunk lost its vigour over the centuries and died off completely. Vestiges of the original trunk can still be seen on the site.

Variations on the elbow style

Multiple elbow style

The three main branches are spread around the main trunk just like elbows. The branch at the back gives depth to the creation. The tree radiates a feeling of otherworldliness.

Root-over-rock elbow style

The main branch cascades down and anchors itself to the ground. The backward curve on the main trunk gives depth to the composition. The rock serves as a background to complement the scene. The apexes of the leaning branch follow the movement of the main trunk, and the two apexes balance the composition. The deep oval or rectangular container accentuates the magnitude of the design.

One-sided elbow style

The tree grows into a slanting position until the main branch eventually touches the ground. It starts rooting and forms a new tree. The movement of the trunk is in the same direction as that of the apex of the branch touching the ground. Avoid crossing trunk lines as they draw the attention away from the beauty of the composition.

Containers

To accommodate the wide-spreading branches, a long oval or rectangular container is recommended. However, should you decide to create the circular 'Wonderboom' style, rather use a round container or a flat stone.

Plant material

Evergreen or deciduous species may be used. Conifers and especially *Ficus* species are highly recommended. In the case of deciduous species those with small leaves tend to produce the best results.

Bibliography

Bartlett's Familiar Quotations, 15th ed., Little Brown & Company, Canada, 1980.

Cleaver, D., *Art, an Introduction*, Harcourt, Brace & World, New York, 1966.

Cox, Skip & Treva, 'Bonsai, Reflective Considerations', *International Bonsai*, Summer/80, New York, 1980.

Gore, F., *Painting: Some basic principles*, Studio Vista, London, 1965.

Hagio, Etsuji, 'Shaping Seed-grown Pine Bonsai – Cascade Style', *International Bonsai*, 1984/No. 3, New York, 1984.

Henegen, Dot, 'Bonsai as Kunsvorm', *Bloemfontein Bonsai Kai*, Herfs 1993, Bloemfontein, South Africa, 1993.

Ito, Seizan, *Forest Bonsai, Handbook on Bonsai Special Techniques*, Special Edition of *Plants & Gardens*, Vol. 22, No. 2, Brooklyn Botanic Garden, Brooklyn, New York, 1966.

Koreshoff, Deborah, R., *Bonsai – Its Art, Science, History and Philosophy*, Boolarang Publications, Brisbane, Australia, 1984.

Lesniewicz, Ilona & Zhimin, Li, *Chinese Bonsai – The Art of Penjing*, Blandford Press, London, 1988.

'Masters Design: Cascade Style – Introduction', *International Bonsai*, 1984/No. 2, New York, 1984.

'Masters Design: Formal Upright Style – Introduction', *International Bonsai*, 1986/No. 2, New York, 1986.

Murata, Kyuzo, *Bonsai Miniature Potted Trees: Their Training and Care for Beginners*, Shufunomoto Co. Ltd, Japan, 1964.

Naka, John Y., Oshima, Mikio, Rosade, F, Chase & Valavanis, William, N., 'Masters Design: Slanting Style and Informal Upright Style – Introduction', *International Bonsai*, 1985/No. 2 & 3, New York, 1985.

Naka, John, Y., *Bonsai Techniques I,* Dennis Landman, California, 1973.

Naka, John, Y., *Bonsai Techniques II,* Dennis Landman, California, 1982.

Nakatsu, Senkichi, 'Slanting Style for the Novice – Part I & II', *International Bonsai*, 1985/No. 2 & 3, New York, 1985.

Palgrave, Keith Coates, *Trees of Southern Africa*, Struik Publishers, Cape Town, 1977.

Palmer, E. & Pitman, N., *Trees of Southern Africa,* 3 Volumes, Balkema, Cape Town, 1972 & 1973.

Petermann, Victoria, 'The Principles of Design in relation to Bonsai', *Cape Bonsai Kai*, Autumn 1994, Cape Town, South Africa, 1994.

Pettito, Andrea, L., 'Is Bonsai Art? Yes, But …, Replies to Yoshimura', *International Bonsai Magazine*, 1993/No. 4, New York, 1993.

Sakakibara, Yoshiro, 'The Visions of the Literati in Literati Paintings', *International Bonsai*, Winter/1981, New York, 1981.

Sausmoret, M., *Basic Design*: *The Dynamics of Visual Form*, Studio Vista, London, 1964.

Suzuki, Saichi, 'Zuisho – Japanese Five Needle Pine', *International Bonsai*, 1991/No. 3, New York, 1991.

Valavanis, William, N., 'Aspects of Bonsai Design –
   Part 1: Trunk line & Direction', Spring/1980,
   Part 2: Silhouette', Summer/1980,
   Part 3: Broom Style', Autumn/1980,
   Part 4: Visual Weight', Winter/1980,
   Part 6: Focal Point (Centre of Interest)', Summer/1981,
   Part 7: Forest Plantings', Autumn/1981,
   Part 8: Literati Style Bonsai', Winter/1981,
   Part 9: Positioning', 1982/No. 1, and
   Part 10: Positioning', 1982/No. 2, *International Bonsai*, New York.

Webster's Third New International Dictionary, Merriam-Webster Inc. Publications, Massachusetts, 1981.

Yamada, Kamajiro, 'Present Day Literati Bonsai', *International Bonsai*, Winter/1981, New York, 1981.

Yoshida, Seiji, 'Fundamentals of Informal Upright Style for Black Pine Bonsai: Part 2', *International Bonsai*, 1983/No. 4, New York, 1984.

Yoshimura Yuji & Halford, Giovanna M., *The Japanese Art of Miniature Trees and Landscapes – their Creation, Care and Enjoyment,* Charles E. Tuttle Company Inc., Rutland, Vermont, 1967.

Yoshimura, Yuji, 'Modern Bonsai – Development of the Art of Bonsai. From an Historical Perspective – Part 2', *International Bonsai*, 1991/No. 4, New York, 1991.

Yoshiroda, Kan, *Bonsai: Japanese Miniature Trees. Their Style, Cultivation and Training*, Faber & Faber, London, 1960.

Glossary

Apex: the highest point of the tree.

Asymmetrical: having two sides or halves that are not the same.

Broad-leafed: relating to plants having broad or relatively broad leaves, for example maple and oak.

Conifer: a tree that bears cones and has needle-like or scale-like leaves; mainly evergreen trees such as pines, cedars, spruces and junipers.

Deciduous: refers to a tree that sheds its foliage at the end of the growing season; maples and elms are examples of deciduous trees.

Driftwood: a style in bonsai that is characterised by the presence of dead wood.

Evergreen: refers to a tree that normally keeps most of its foliage through the winter; pines and yellowwoods are examples of evergreen trees.

Hardwood: the wood from a broad-leafed tree (such as oak, ash or beech) as distinguished from that of conifers.

Jin: the Japanese term for a dead tip on a branch or trunk; jins are artificially created from unwanted branches by stripping the bark and cambium to represent dead wood.

Lime sulphur: a chemical used to preserve dead wood (jins and shari's); it prevents infection and also bleaches the stripped branch or trunk in order to mature the jin or shari.

Negative space: the 'empty space' between solid elements such as branches or foliage, or the space that surrounds the bonsai; it helps to define the boundaries of positive space and brings balance to the composition.

Shari: the Japanese term used for the area where the bark and cambium have been removed from a branch or trunk to give the appearance of a mature tree that struggled against the elements (wind, lightning, ice, etc.).

Silhouette: a two-dimensional representation of the outline or general shape of the tree.

Small-leafed: relating to plants having needle-like or simple leaves, for example conifers or olive trees.

Softwood: the wood from a conifer (such as pine, fir or spruce) as distinguished from that of broad-leafed trees.

Symmetrical: a tree is symmetrical if it has corresponding similar parts, i.e. one side is the same as the other.

Japanese terms and the English equivalent

Amayadori-ishi – shelter from rain rock

Bankan – gnarled trunk style

Bunjin – literati / free form style

Chokkan – formal upright / straight trunk / cedar-tree style

Dai-kengai – vertical cascade

Dai-shakan – extreme slant

Dan-ishi – sentinel rock

Fuki-nagashi – windswept style

Gohan-yose – five-tree style

Gokan – five-trunk style

Goza-kake – elongated branch style

Han-kengai – semi-cascade style

Hoki-zukuri – broom style

Hu-shakan – medium slant

Ikadabuki – fallen tree style

Ishi-zuke – clinging-to-the-rock style

Kabudachi – clump/sprout style

Kaminari – struck-by-lightning style

Karame-miki – plaited / entwined trunk style

Kasa-zukuri – wild fig style

Kengai – cascade style

Kobukan – knobby trunk style

Korabuki – turtle-back / stump style

Kyuhan-yose – nine-tree style

Kyukan – nine-trunk style

Matsu-zukuri – pine-tree style

Moyo-gi – informal upright style

Nanakan – seven-trunk style

Nanakan-yose – seven-tree style

Ne-agari – exposed root style

Nejikan – coiled / spiral / twisted trunk style

Netsuranari – root-connected / sinuous style

Pien-tshu – plaited / entwined trunk style

Rosoku-zukuri – candle-flame style

Ryu-ho – dragon/phoenix

Sabakan – hollow trunk style

Saba-miki – hollow trunk style

Saikai – planted landscape

Samon-yose – triple-tree style

Sankan – triple-trunk style

Seki-jo-ju – root-over-rock style

Shakan – slanting style

Sharikan – peeled bark style

Shari-miki – driftwood style

Shidare-zukuri – willow / weeping style

Shima gata – island rock

Shizen-zukuri – bushveld / natural style

Sho-shakan – moderate slant

Sogu-ki – split trunk style

Soju – twin-tree style

Sokan – double-trunk style

Tachiki – informal upright style

Takan-kengai – twin-/triple-trunk cascade

Taki-ishi – waterfall

Taki-kengai – waterfall cascade

Tako-zukuri – octopus style

Tatami-mat – elongated branch style

Toyama – distant mountain

Tsukomi-yose – fist arrangement / cone style

Yama-yori – fist arrangement / cone style

Yose-uye – group / forest plantings

Index

Page numbers in *italics* refer to photographs.